The
Di...
C...
Directing

Edited by
Stephen Peithman
Neil Offen

HEINEMANN
Portsmouth, NH

For all those in front of the lights and behind the scenes
who understand the magic of theater

HEINEMANN
A division of Reed Elsevier Inc.
361 Hanover Street
Portsmouth, NH 03801–3912
http://www.heinemanndrama.com

Offices and agents throughout the world

The editors and publisher wish to thank those who have generously given permission to reprint borrowed material:

"You Want to Do a Play About WHAT?" by Jerome McDonough originally appeared in the catalogue of I. E. Clark Publications. Reprinted by permission of the Publisher.

"Putting on the Dog" by Mary Johnson originally appeared in *Stage Directions* (April 1996). Copyright © by Mary Johnson. Reprinted by permission of the Author.

LIBRARY OF CONGRESS CATALOGING-IN-PUBLICATION DATA
The Stage directions guide to directing / edited by Stephen Peithman,
    Neil Offen.
        p.   cm.
    ISBN 0-325-00112-X
    1. Theater—Production and direction.   I. Peithman, Stephen.
II. Offen, Neil.   III. Stage directions (West Sacramento, Calif.)
PN2053.S675   1999
792'.0233—dc21   98-56058
                                                                           CIP

Editor: Lisa A. Barnett
Production: Abigail M. Heim
Cover design: Barbara Werden
Cover photo: Rob Karosis
Manufacturing: Louise Richardson

Printed in the United States of America on acid-free paper

03   02   01   00   99   DA   1   2   3   4   5

Contents

Foreword

Directors are the unseen presence in stage productions, yet their influence is everywhere to be seen—and heard.

Like the captain of a ship, the director is always on watch to make sure the vessel reaches its destination. To expand the analogy, there are many workers below decks, each with his or her own task, but it's ultimately the captain's role to meld these people into a successful team. And, like the audience in a theater, the ship's passengers seldom see the hard work that goes on behind the scenes, because the emphasis is always on helping them enjoy the voyage.

There are differences, of course. The most obvious one is that, in the theater, the voyage is different each time—a different play, a different audience, a different cast, a different interpretation. And, unlike the good director, the captain of a ship is the perfect model of a top-down management style. It's difficult to conceive of an officer asking a crew member, "Well, how do *you* want to get to Bermuda this time?"

In contrast, the nature of theater is creative and collaborative, and the director of a play always must juggle expediency with artistic purpose, production issues with human psychology. And because each voyage is different, there's no one way to run this particular ship.

However, there *are* many ideas and tools at a director's disposal, many of which you'll find in this book. In *The Stage Directions Guide to Directing*, the editors of *Stage Directions* magazine have blended our own knowledge and experience in directing with the expertise of veteran directors and actors in community, regional, and academic theater.

After an overview of the director's role, the book focuses on how the director shapes and guides a production from preproduction meetings to curtain call. (We have touched on the director's involvement in the audition process only briefly here; however, you'll find a complete treatment in *The Stage Directions Guide to Auditions*.)

Whether you are a veteran of many productions or a newcomer to the stage, we hope *The Stage Directions Guide to Directing* provides you with the tools you need to guide your ship and unlock the potential of the plays you choose to direct.

About Stage Directions *and This Book*

The majority of the material in this book is based on information that first appeared in the pages of *Stage Directions*, the "practical magazine of theater." Since 1988, *Stage Directions* has published articles on a wide variety of subject matter—not only acting and directing, but also management, publicity, scenic and costume design, lighting and special effects, and much more.

During that time, we've taken a close look at almost every aspect of the directing process. We've put all that advice together in this book, updated and revised as needed, and added introductions that help put the information into perspective.

As we do with our magazine, we'd like to hear your comments on this book or suggestions for future topics in our expanding library of *Stage Directions* books. Please write to us at: *Stage Directions*, 3101 Poplarwood Court, Suite 310, Raleigh, NC 27604.

Stephen Peithman, Editor-in-Chief
Neil Offen, Editor

Introduction

*T*he Romans had a word for it: *dirigere*, meaning to lay straight or point the way. That word, in turn, is a combination of the Latin *di* (apart, from) and *regere* (to rule). So the word *dirigere*—from which our word *director* has evolved—refers to someone who stands apart from the action and points the way.

If only it were that simple.

And, in fact, at one time it was. Before 1900, for example, the director's function was handled by the actor-manager. Henry Irving, among many others, directed his own productions in London from 1878 to 1901. In other cases, the author directed. In others, plays were directed by the theater manager, who often was a theatrical businessman.

In all cases, however, there has to be someone in charge of rehearsals, just as there has to be someone in charge of any cooperative activity.

"At rehearsals, someone must act as chairman of the proceedings," said director Tyrone Guthrie, "to arbitrate conflicting interests, to unify conflicting ideas of interpretation, even to initiate ideas. In the interests of efficiency, this person must at rehearsal be accorded the same sort of authority which is accorded to the chairman of a business or political meeting."

In the real world of theater, the director is seen less as a chairman than as the holder of the artistic vision that guides the production. In so doing, the director may act as leader or dictator. Collaborative or proscriptive. Mentor or nudge. Preacher or psychologist.

In fact, there are many facets to the directorial role, and these are further complicated by the different personality of each director—not to mention the personalities of the actors, designers, and even of the plays themselves. Clearly, there can be no one way to deal with all this and, in fact, most directors find they use a variety of approaches, depending on the situation, the play, the cast, the crew.

What makes a good director? Because the director is in charge of a given production, there is a great need for a strong overview of theater. An effective director needs study or experience in acting, stagecraft, lighting, costuming, makeup, theater history, dance and stage movement, and psychology. In addition, you need to know a great deal about dramatic literature to select plays wisely or accept an assignment if asked.

As a director, you normally are responsible for staging the play, coaching the actors, and making sure all the elements of the production are integrated. To ensure artistic unity, the director must be the final authority in all matters related to the production. But "authority" does not mean being a dictator. It means that you develop a unified artistic vision of the show, that you communicate it clearly with your production staff and actors, and that you allow them to find creative methods of supporting that vision. "Final authority" really means that if there are questions of appropriateness that cannot be resolved by staff, the director will make the final determination.

Other members of a production team might include a technical director, lighting designer, costume designer, scenic designer, and stage manager. Some teams also include a makeup designer, choreographer, musical director, property head, and crew chiefs for stage, lighting, makeup, sound, house, and publicity.

To make sure the team proceeds with its work effectively, you'll need to have preproduction meetings to share your vision of the show, to determine the budget, to ensure that rights to the play are cleared and the theater is booked, and to schedule a series of conferences with production staff members. You'll also want to set the dates and times for auditions. (For this subject, see *The Stage Directions Guide to Auditions*.)

The director takes the lead at the first production conference. Here, you present your interpretation of the play and your concept of the production's style or look. The designers will have a chance to react to your ideas, enlarge on them, or even suggest a different approach. Listen carefully. Their ideas may alter the way you see the play. On the other hand, if you decide to proceed with your original concept, try to incorporate as much as possible the best ideas of your staff.

A second conference is called after designers have had a chance to mull over the ideas expressed at the first meeting. Preliminary sketches of set, costume, or lighting designs are presented and talked over to see how they mesh with the director's vision and support each other.

A third meeting looks at revised designs, color sketches, and scale models of the sets. If this is a musical, the choreographer needs to be present to see if any of the designs conflict with practical concerns of stage movement. At this point, all involved should have a good sense of what the show will look like so they can continue to refine their concepts and designs.

The director should continue to confer with technical staff throughout the production period. However, these conferences should not occur during rehearsal, when a director should be concentrating on working with the actors. This, indeed, is the most crucial part of the director's job and, not surprisingly, makes up the bulk of this book.

Earlier we asked, "What makes a good director?" Aside from training, good instincts, intelligence, and organization, a director must be able to create an artistic vision of the play and then communicate that vision effectively to cast and production staff. It's a tall order, but it's done every day.

So . . . let's get started.

PREPRODUCTION

PART

I

1 | Ten Steps for Picking the Right Play

What to Look for Before You Decide

When a production goes well, praise usually goes to the acting, directing, scenic design, and costumes. But the real reason these elements work so well together is that the play itself fits the performing group's capabilities. Sometimes, finding the right play is fortuitous. But more often, it's a case of careful thought.

In some companies, plays are chosen by a committee, or an artistic director, as part of a season, without the input of directors. In others, however, the directors do have input—and in some cases, may do all the selecting. Whichever is true in your situation, here's how to make good choices more consistently—by your responses to the following questions.

1. *Is it a good play?* This may sound elementary, but people choose plays for all sorts of reasons. The script must provide a strong story, interesting characters, well-written dialogue, an important theme or entertaining approach, and that intangible "something" that makes a show intriguing to watch.

2. *Is the play appropriate for your audience?* Consider who is likely to attend. Will they understand it? Will they approve of its message or language? Or will it try to reshape their attitudes? Controversy in and of itself is not a good reason for selecting a play. You want to stir your audience, of course, but not necessarily offend them. After all, you do want them to return.

3. *Can you cast the play?* Consider not only individual actors who might take roles if offered, but also whether the percentage of males and females reflects your group or the pool of actors available to you. If you have a preponderance of women and you want to produce a musical, you would be wiser to choose *The Sound of Music* rather than *1776*. Does the play depend on one major role played brilliantly? *Auntie Mame* and *The Matchmaker* need strong female leads, while *You Can't Take It with You* and *Glengarry Glen Ross* are ensemble shows. Which type of show is best for you?

4. *Can you handle the play's technical requirements?* How many sets are required? How realistic do they need to be? Do you have room to store sets off stage when not in use? Are there special lighting or sound requirements? Special effects? If you can't fly your Peter Pan, perhaps you ought to look elsewhere for a show.

5. *Can you easily (and affordably) costume the show?* Period shows, such as *Oklahoma!* or *The Imaginary Invalid,* demand much more time and money than plays set in contemporary America.

6. *Can you afford the play*? Royalties can be expensive, as can costumes and sets. Calculate a rough budget in your head as you consider a particular play. Does it match the average expenses for shows you're doing now or is it a quantum leap into the unknown?

7. *Is the play available?* Surprisingly, not all plays you might want to produce are available, particularly the newest ones or those being revived at major theaters in New York or other areas of the country. Check with the play publisher to be sure.

8. *Does the play fit with the rest of your season?* Most successful companies alternate comedy and drama, old and new, musical and nonmusical. That way they can balance their offerings and build audiences.

9. *Is the play one that will appeal* to actors, designers, and production staff? If it doesn't excite their imagination, it's not likely to get the psychological and hands-on support it needs to succeed.

10. *Do you really want to do the show?* Avoid directing anything that you would not have chosen yourself. Enthusiasm for a project is all-important.

2 | *Finding the Right Play for You*

How do you find the right play when you have mostly female or male actors? No one to build elaborate sets? A cast all over the age of fifty? A minuscule budget—or stage?

The answers may lie in the most obvious place—catalogues of plays. Most actually make it fairly simple to find plays that meet your requirements. You will find a complete list of play publishers on the Stage Directions *website at <www.stage-directions. com>, on the "SD+" menu.*

How to Use Play Catalogues to Guide the Way

"*T*his year we purchased forty-eight scripts at $6 each," a reader wrote *Stage Directions*. "We hope to select four to stage. To date, we have rejected twenty-seven and accepted two. When you consider the cost and time, we wasted a great deal. The play catalogues offer only brief descriptions and many are a bit misleading. How can you know what's good? They do not have a rating system that would let us know about offensive or just plain boring content. One script sounded great, but turned out to be very offensive and a bit boring. On the other hand, we almost missed another that turned out to be wonderful. What is 'offensive' to us? Well, we are very liberal on stage left and very conservative on stage right. We have had *The Normal Heart* and *Catch Me If You Can,* as well as melodrama and murders. But how do we know when looking in the catalogues? How can we learn to read catalogues better?"

It's important not to expect more from catalogues than they were intended to deliver. They are, after all, sales pieces, not critical commentary. And even if play catalogues *did* provide critical commentary, whose judgment would it reflect? How would it correlate with your taste, your audience, your community, and your strengths (or weaknesses) as a theater company? The truth is, only you know what will work best for your theater and your audience. No one else can determine that for you.

What a play catalogue *can* do is tell you that a play is available and from whom, as well as give you a plot outline, cast breakdown, and something about length and set requirements. It's unrealistic to ask for more.

To cut down the time spent on reading unsuitable plays, you need to do your homework first. There are two ways to do this.

The first approach is to read the catalogues and create a list of the plays that may be worth reading. Then find out if they have been reviewed in national magazines or major metropolitan newspapers. Publications to check include *Stage Directions, American Theatre, Dramatics*, and general-interest magazines such as *Time* and *Newsweek, The New Yorker*, and of course, the *New York Times*. Other resources are *The Best Plays* annuals and the bound volumes of the New York drama critics reviews. Your nearest research or large public library should be able to help you; smaller libraries should be able to get these sources through interlibrary loan. You also can search the World Wide Web to find out what other companies are producing. You'll find a list of community theater companies, for example, on the website of the American Association of Community Theatre at <www.aact.org>.

A second approach is to keep an ongoing card (or computer) file of plays as you read about them in these same consumer publications. Then, when you see these plays appear in the catalogues, you can consult your file. The advantage here is that the file will contain only those plays you *know* are of interest to you.

What about plays that have not been produced or for which you cannot find reviews? One answer is to find out as much as you can about the playwright. If he or she has a strong reputation for other plays, chances are good that this one at least will be worth consideration.

[We should point out that *Stage Directions'* "New Plays" department lists only those plays we feel merit your attention, not every play published. Besides the basic information you'll find in a catalogue, you'll also get our honest reaction to the content and potential acting, audience, and technical challenges. You also should check our cumulative article index to see if the play was reviewed in a back issue.]

Finally, encourage company members to read widely and stay informed about new plays and theater in general. Go to as many plays as you can. Seeing one play by an unknown playwright can tell you something about other works by the same person. Keep up with the productions other groups in your region are doing and share information with them. Join your regional theater alliance—or help start one.

Play selection is not an exact science, but armed with more information, you can reduce frustration and increase your chances for success.

Thirteen Reasons Not to Pick a Show

A Baker's Dozen of Common Traps and How to Avoid Them

No theater company sets out to make a bad choice. Still, it happens. After all, choosing a play or a season depends on making informed choices that balance many often competing needs. It's a complex process and one that demands thought and deliberation.

Any one of the following thirteen reasons might be justified as *one* consideration in choosing a play. We've all heard them in discussions about an upcoming season. We court disaster only when we focus on one of them to the exclusion of all others.

1. *"We have a director who wants to do it."* Without a committed director, a production is almost sure to fail. But directors are not always good judges of what is best for your theater or what will appeal to your audience. For example, most directors have "wish lists" of plays they've never had the chance to do. Often there's a good reason—the play presents serious problems. However, when a director loves a play that much, he or she may not have a clear-eyed view of the project. Ultimately, your choice should be one that your actors, technical crew, support staff, and patrons will back as well.

2. *"We owe the director a favor."* We know of three cases where this was the rationale. In two instances, the results were less than successful because the directors used this as leverage, insisting on doing a show from their "wish list" (see Number 1).

3. *"It's cheap."* We all want to save money, but cheap at what price? The cost of producing a play should be considered, of course, but if audiences stay away, the money you spend is wasted whether the cost is great or small. There are many fine plays available for little or no royalty fees; there are also fine plays with sizeable royalties or high production costs. Your choice should satisfy both artistic and commercial needs.

4. *"We've already got the costumes"* or its variant, *"It's a one-set show."* See Number 3.

5. *"We can cast it with the folks we have."* It's a good idea to consider plays in light of the actors who work with your company. On the other hand, if you always cast shows with the same actors, should you instead consider something that will pull in new people?

6. *"It's an important play."* Important to whom? Tread carefully here: The didactic impulse can be a strong one, but it is not the best reason to choose a play. Perhaps the audience *should* see it, but will they stay away instead? Worse, perhaps, is an "important" play that is beyond the capabilities of your company. Not only does the audience lose, but so does the playwright and, ultimately, your company's reputation. Whether a play is "important" or not, it must hold the interest of your audience.

7. *"It's well known."* While it's true that familiar shows are easier to sell, they do come with their own baggage. Expectations are higher when audiences know the show in question. Will they be disappointed if your version doesn't live up to their memory of the film or another stage version? The play's notoriety also may present problems in casting, sets, lighting, costuming, or special effects. Other factors also may affect its success: We recall a production of *Guys and Dolls* that was beautifully mounted and critically praised— and that played to half-empty houses. It was produced in a university town in the summer.

8. *"It's by a well-known playwright."* This can be a plus, but it's no guarantee. Even Neil Simon has had his failures. And could you promote Shakespeare's *Henry VIII* to your patrons as easily as *Romeo and Juliet*? Could you mount as good a production of the former as the latter? More important, is the play worth doing at all?

9. *"We've done it before."* It's tempting to repeat something that was successful in the past, but you risk comparisons with the earlier production. Can you cast it as well as the last time? And has your audience changed in the intervening period?

10. *"Our audiences want it."* Unfortunately, people often say one thing and then do quite another. For example, surveys indicated that most television viewers believed there was too much being broadcast about the O.J. Simpson trial and President Clinton scandals, but ratings proved otherwise. Likewise, when one professional theater company asked its patrons which musicals they wanted to see, the answer was "new and different" ones; the resulting season was a disaster. While it's important to get feedback from your audience, compare it with your own experience of what types of shows draw the crowds and schedule accordingly.

11. *"The theater company in the next city did it and it was a hit."* Theater companies are different. So are audiences. So are actors, directors, sets, costumes, and publicity people. Beware of facile comparisons.

12. *"It's the best we could come up with."* Unfortunately, *best* here doesn't translate as *highest quality* but rather as *least objectionable.* How can your company get behind such a show with all the energy needed to make it a success?

13. *"It's safe."* Don't confuse "risk-taking" with foolhardiness. A *calculated* risk is one in which you have weighed the options and determined that you have more to gain from something new and different than by remaining static. If you can mount a high-quality production of a particular play and it presents no threat to your company's finances, why not consider it? If you do only "safe" shows, you do neither yourself nor your audiences a favor.

Show selection is a fine art. The decision must consider your company's resources—human, physical, and fiscal—as well as your audience and artistic goals.

4 | *Seven Reasons Not to Attempt the Classics*

. . . And All the Reasons Why We Should, Anyway

Dale Lyles

We've all heard the reasons why it's not a good idea for your small, struggling theater to take on Shakespeare, or Molière, or any of the other classic playwrights and plays. The reasons, I think, boil down to seven specifics. Here they are—and here are all the reasons why you shouldn't pay any attention to them.

1. *They are too hard to costume.* The clothing of the past is too elaborate to reproduce. There are too many pieces, no patterns available, and nobody knows how to make them. Costuming a period show also is too expensive, because of the cost of each costume and the size of the cast.

Well, no one says you have to do a show in its original period. Shakespeare is famous for being easy to reset into more amenable periods. (Make sure, though, that the period in which you reset it relates to the play. It wouldn't make sense to set the wild and woolly *The Taming of the Shrew* in the cool, cerebral eighteenth century just because you have costumes left over from *DuBarry Was a Lady.*)

But many period plays can be transferred into distant

settings. At the Newnan Community Theatre Company in Georgia, we did *A Comedy of Errors* in which all the characters wore gray sweatsuits. Not only did the twins look alike—*everyone* looked alike. Each character wore a differently colored face paint; the twins, of course, matched. The result was an extremely physical style of *commedia* performance. Audiences howled at the comedy, didn't miss the doublets.

If you can do it, the joys of period costuming usually outweigh the frustrations. There is something glorious about putting together a world that looks and feels differently than yours. Even if you don't go for precise historical accuracy—and who can afford all that brocade and trim?—the experience is good to have, both for your costumers and your actors. Our *The Winter's Tale* was a soul-fulfilling experience for the entire company. What a thrill when the entire court appeared on stage in full Elizabethan regalia.

2. *The sets are too complicated.* These plays call for multiple sets in architectural styles that are far too ornate for us. The time, talent, and budget required are all more than we can handle.

Obviously, the complaint cannot be true about Shakespeare, because his plays were written to be performed without sets at all. But what can one do about, say, Feydeau's *A Flea in Her Ear*, with its Act One drawing room; its Act Two sleazy hotel with staircases, cutaway rooms, and revolving beds; and its return to the drawing room in Act Three? Or worse, *She Stoops to Conquer*, with a tavern, multiple locations within a household, and an overturned coach in a garden?

If your group is like mine, you can devote your resources either to elaborate sets or to elaborate costumes, or neither, but not to both. Instead, focus on the costumes and cut back on the sets: a simple chair or a single window is often enough to define the space for an audience. The audience always will focus on the actors, so costumes are more important.

Again, if you feel like replicating the actual period, go for it. We once did *Tartuffe*, for which the director requested and got a replica of a seventeenth-century theater, with raked stage, forced perspective, and elaborately painted surfaces. (Was it a lot of work? You bet—it was this production that convinced us to simplify for *A Comedy of Errors* three months later.)

3. *The language is too hard to deal with.* Tackling all those long sentences and strange words is just too daunting for an actor. And don't even talk about verse!

The truth is that there is no such thing as an actor who can't, only an actor who won't. If your actors have talent, then the rest of it is a learning process.

But who will teach it? There are plenty of books on acting Shakespeare, especially, as well as videotapes, and there are more than a few books on acting other periods. Buy them, read them, practice them. Build on what you read, however, keeping in mind what you know to be effective within your own group.

When we perform Shakespeare, I set aside a sizeable chunk of rehearsal time for workshops and learning how to "do" Shakespeare. The result is that we have never had a problem casting our Shakespeares; for *The Winter's Tale*, I had more than forty people audition for the twenty or so slots because they were excited about the chance to perform these marvelous texts. They have discovered that the language is not your enemy; it is your best tool. And what an amazing tool it is!

4. *Nobody knows or understands the production styles of past periods*. Our director and designers don't have a clue about how the plays of Molière and Shakespeare were staged. The scripts don't help either, without a floor plan in the back and stage directions in parentheses.

So who says you have to do it precisely as they did? Discover it for yourself. Make it work for you. Make it work for your audiences.

Research, learn, create. You want to do *The Imaginary Invalid* set in a hyper-modern sterile environment? Go for it. You want to put *The Taming of the Shrew* in the Wild West? Do it. You want to set *The Pirates of Penzance* in 1930s Hollywood? We're doing it.

5. *Our actors do not have the training to do these antiques*. Local actors cannot possibly measure up to the standards familiar to audiences through such movies as *Richard III*. They've never done these kinds of plays and wouldn't know how to begin.

Of course they know how to begin. They begin by reading the script, learning lines, fleshing out the character, exploring through rehearsal and endless experiment. How else would they begin? Who says you have to have been to Stratford or Juilliard to know how to begin these things?

As far as measuring up to Emma Thompson and Kenneth Branagh, who can? But that doesn't mean your production is neither enjoyable nor worthwhile. How many times have you had audience members tell you that they had seen the same show on Broadway and enjoyed yours so much more? Truthfully, do you think that your production was more polished than the professional Broadway production? Probably not, but if the audience enjoyed it, they enjoyed it.

Besides, every show ought to stretch the company's members in some way. They will appreciate it.

6. *These plays do not have the audience appeal that modern plays do.* Great works? No, they're too long, boring, obscure, elitist, and esoteric. Our audiences would not come to see them, and if they did, they wouldn't be happy.

That has not been our experience. If you pick Strindberg's *Dream Play*, then you deserve what you get, I guess, but if you start out with the "safe picks" like *A Midsummer Night's Dream*, *A Comedy of Errors, Tartuffe,* and any Feydeau, the audience will have as much fun with them as they would with any other well-produced script. Overheard in the parking lot after our production of *Twelfth Night:* "That was really funny. Who wrote that?" (That production, by the way, was done in a bare room, costumed in contemporary beach-resort attire entirely made of hand-painted muslin.)

7. *These plays would be too much work and not enough fun.* With all these difficult problems, it's not worth our time and energy to tackle one of these great works. All we'd be doing is beating our head against the wall for no good reason.

No actors or technical people have ever dropped out of one of our Shakespeares because they weren't enjoying it. And always they ask, "What's the next one?"

We've come to feel over the years that even if we don't achieve perfection, even if our *The Winter's Tale* is not the Royal Shakespeare Company's, still we will have climbed higher than if we had selected some safe but minor script.

Indeed, as time goes by, you'll find your company has become more "athletic" with the exercise and will be less likely to tolerate second-rate scripts. We all have only so much time; why waste it doing bad stuff?

Get thee to thy library and read a classic. Plan it. Create it. Do it.

5 | How to Read a Script

You've checked out catalogues and gotten information about a particular play or playwright. You've narrowed down your choices somewhat. Now comes the hard part: focusing on the work itself and making the final selection. Here's how to do it.

Ten Ways to Judge Whether a Play Is Right for You

JIM DE YOUNG

A play belongs on a stage, not on a page. Yet, for most of us who select a season's productions, the only convenient or available way of experiencing a script is to read it. This is particularly true when we're faced with the problem of selecting one script from a dozen or more possibilities. The challenge is to construct a potential performance vividly in your imagination as you read.

As Kenneth Thorpe Rowe writes in *A Theatre in Your Head*, you must see the scene of the play in your mind's eye, populate that scene with living characters who move within it, hear the dialogue in your ears, and feel the created tensions and emotions of the characters. Reading a play, Rowe writes, "demands active projection of imagination."

Here are ten rules that can lead you to a more useful, efficient, entertaining, and high-quality reading of a play.

1. *Select a suitable environment.* Your reading environment should approximate the theater experience. This means a quiet space reasonably protected from interruptions. There should be neither blaring music nor television, no telephones ringing every other minute, and no expectation of a revolving-door parade of visitors.

2. *Read it in one sitting.* Interrupt your reading only at the stated act breaks. You want to give yourself a sustained sense of the basic continuity, mood, theme, and characters just as you or another audience member might experience them in the theater. If you are reading a script for formal analysis or an academic critique, you would want to reread and study it more closely, but most spectators will see a production straight through and see it only once. If the play does not communicate something of interest to you on a first uninterrupted reading, what leads you to believe it will communicate something to an audience?

3. *Design a setting.* Read the opening stage directions carefully and take some time to visualize the environment. Create a theater space in your mind and put an imagined setting for the play on the stage of your imagination. Think of your own theater space, its advantages and limitations, and how this play might work there.

4. *Create the technical elements.* Continue to read the stage directions throughout the play. Look for other technical clues. Color in your mental picture of the illumination of the scene, how the characters are dressed, and what they are carrying, holding, or using. When you are reading a play, it is easy to skip over the visual descriptions under the mistaken assumption that the words are the most important element. When you are actually in a theater, the physical setting, the changing lights, the color of the costumes always are visible and provide powerful and constant elaboration of the words you hear. Visualize not only the possibilities, but how your particular designers and technicians would deal with the play's technical demands.

5. *See the actors' moves.* As you read the dialogue, move the characters about in your imagined setting. Keep track of when and where they enter and with whom they congregate or from whom they detach themselves. Notice when and where and with whom they exit. These are the building blocks of conflicts and relationships.

6. *Make a playmark.* If character names and basic relationships give you trouble, jot them down on a piece of paper like a bookmark. Let this item travel with you from page to page. This is especially helpful when the play has a large cast.

7. *Mark areas for further study or review.* Have a pencil handy to mark points that you may wish to return to later, but do not reread passages as you move through the script. An audience member

can't stand up and call for a rerun of the scene during a performance; you should not indulge yourself at this time either.

8. *Listen to and watch the characters.* Work to perceive the tone of the speeches and the pantomime or facial characteristics inherent in them. In other words, try to see the characters reacting and hear the dialogue in your ear. If you find this difficult, you might try to read a speech or two aloud from each character to get your ear attuned to the emotion and the rhythm and/or cadences of the various speakers.

9. *Review the experience at the end.* When you finish reading the play, carry on a dialogue with yourself much as you might talk with a knowledgeable friend about the show immediately after seeing it. What did you like best and/or least about it? What was it like? What were the dominant colors, textures, patterns, temperatures, sounds, and moods? What was the playwright trying to say? Did the piece fit into a standard literary genre? Which elements of the drama (for example, plot, character, theme, dialogue, scenic spectacle, music) were emphasized in the play? Which were handled effectively? Did the work strike your fancy or keep your attention right up to the very end?

If this conversation is not enjoyable and generally positive, do you really wish to spend five or six more weeks with this work?

10. *Know the theatrical background.* When reading plays, particularly those written in or about the past, your ability to understand and picture the action in your mind's eye is helped if you have an adequate historical perspective. Reading the author's other works and reading about the artistic environment of the piece, the theatrical conventions of the period, and the physical theater where the play originally was performed helps you appreciate and understand the ambiance of a script. If this information is not already a part of your general knowledge, you should make it a component of your reading.

The application of these simple rules will help you reproduce a more vivid theatrical performance in your head as you read a play. It is a skill that all those who evaluate plays should strive to acquire. It's also one that can afford the casual reader of playscripts increased pleasure as well.

Is It Legal to Change the Script?

All right, you've chosen the play you want to direct. You like it very much, except, well, there's that scene in Act Two. And the monologue that's supposed to be the play's climax really goes on much too long, you feel. Yes, it's the play you want, but you'd like to make just a few changes. Can you?

*I*n most cases of copyrighted plays, the answer is no.

Most playwrights oppose changes in the text and protection against this is stated in the contract you sign when you negotiate the rights. Cuts or changes in dialogue may seem minor to the director, but easily can alter the author's intentions. In most cases, the license states clearly that the play must be performed as written.

This does not mean that changes are impossible, merely that you must check with the publisher/agent to clear them before you put them into effect.

Indeed, most publishers *urge* directors to contact them regarding possible changes, because there may be an accommodation. The key to acceptance is how the change affects the integrity of the script. Playwrights and their agents are reasonable people, and if your request makes sense, it may be granted. However, note that most requests are handled on an individual basis. In many cases, the playwright or the playwright's estate must be contacted for permission.

One recent addition to licenses is a "gender clause," which restricts changing a character's sex from female to male or vice versa. This grew out of a lawsuit won by the publisher

Tams-Witmark in which a company changed the gender of Reno Sweeney in *Anything Goes* from female to male. Considering that Reno has a romance with a British gentleman in the show, the sex change put an entirely new slant on the plot.

Because changes are not a black-and-white situation, it's a good idea to be certain about them before you present the play.

"Always ask," says Aileen Hussung of Samuel French. "It never hurts to ask."

Make your requests as specific as possible, says Craig Pospisil of Dramatists Play Service. "Don't write and ask to 'cut a little bit' out of Act One. Be specific about the cuts, including the specific words and lines and pages."

As you might expect by this point, there is no across-the-board formula regarding excerpting or cutting plays for competition or similar uses.

"You can't cut or excerpt Albee, Beckett, or Williams," says Pospisil. "Others may allow it, but each request has to be checked with the author or his estate."

All the representatives we talked with agree it is easier to get approval to do just one act rather than cut down an entire play to fit a time constraint.

Substitutions is another issue.

"Composers get livid when you put in songs from the movie version," says Music Theater International's Steve Spiegel. "And rightly so, since you are altering their work."

In most cases, you are not allowed to substitute or add songs in a musical. For example, because many people are most familiar with the film version of *Grease*, many directors are tempted to add songs written for the movie. This violates the license. (The recent national touring and Broadway version, however, has negotiated rights to the movie songs.) When a university theater company asked to add the song "If You Go Away" to the score of *Jacques Brel Is Alive and Well and Living in Paris,* the request was denied.

Such substitutions aren't always caught. Charles Tweed of the Jewel Box Theater in Oklahoma City reports that when the conductor's rental score of *Funny Girl* arrived, he discovered a previous user had drawn a line through the first page of the overture (which begins with "Don't Rain on My Parade") and written "Substitute 'My Man,' " a song used in the film but not in the original Broadway production.

Royalties, rights, and licensing are integral elements in the process of presenting plays to the public. It's true the rules are not always clear, mostly because each playwright works out the rules separately for each play. It's also true most publisher/agents want to make it as easy as possible for you to license their productions. After all, they make their money by doing so.

This means you do have some leverage. So work with the publisher from the get-go. If you have questions, ask. If you are considering changes, ask. If you have a problem, explain. After all, we're all in this together.

7 | *Photocopying Plays*

You're fairly certain about your play selection, but would like others to take a look at the work you've chosen. Or perhaps after you've made the selection, you want to get to work on the production with your scenic and lighting designers. The easiest way to do this, you think, simply would be to make a photocopy of the play. But before you do so, listen to what play publishers have to say.

Publishers Explain What's Legal and What Isn't

*I*t's done every day. And for the most part, it's illegal.

We're talking about the photocopying of scripts—rented, purchased, or borrowed. It's a confusing area to most, so we asked play publishers to shed some light on what is permissible and what isn't, and what options there are.

We sent questionnaires to a cross section of the royalty business, from small to large. We presented them with five scenarios, drawn from real-life situations in community, academic, and regional theater. Ten publishers answered our questionnaire: Anchorage Press, Baker's Plays, Broadway Play Publishing, Contemporary Drama Services, Eldridge Publishing Co., Encore Performance Publishing, I.E. Clark, Music Theatre International, Pioneer Drama Service, and Samuel French. We thank each of them for their participation.

While there was general agreement on some of the issues raised by our scenarios, in some cases there were also significant differences in policy. This only underscores how important it is for a director (as well as a producer) to read—and understand—copyright and contractual language. When in doubt, request permission.

Here are the scenarios and publisher comments.

SCENARIO ONE: *A community theater company's play-selection committee will be reading scripts as possible productions for the next season. To expedite the selection process, photocopies of each play are routed to members of the committee.*

Score: Yes: 0   No: 10   Maybe: 0

The response was unanimous on this one: All said no. Said Clark: "Making copies of copyrighted material is illegal unless permission in writing is received from the publisher/agent. We would not give permission in this case." "That is what our preview copies are for," said Contemporary Drama. "They are inexpensive and may be easily ordered for a committee." Music Theatre International: "We allow for each script to be held for a three-week period on perusal. This time period allows for all parties to read each script." Eldridge took a slightly different tack: "Surely the play committee can buy several copies that committee members may take turns reading." And in a similar vein is Pioneer's comment: "If there are several people involved in the selection process and they did not leave sufficient time to circulate copies among themselves, then they need to purchase multiple reading copies." Enlarging on this, Encore suggested that most companies can afford several copies of plays for reading purposes. "If you choose not to do the play," it says, "donate the copies to a library or school, or keep them on hand for future decisions. Or donate to a theater organization. The Ohio Community Theatre Association maintains a library of loaner scripts for this reason, available to all its members statewide." So do many regional theater alliances.

SCENARIO TWO: *A company has received perusal copies of a script and orchestral scores of a musical and decides to do the show. Production dates are mid-November, and arrival date for the materials is eight weeks prior to opening. However, the musical director wants to work with the cast on the music over the summer months, so he photocopies the perusal score. (The company has already sent in a check for royalty and rental.)*

Score: Yes: 1   No: 7   Maybe: 0   Not Applicable: 2

Only one company, Contemporary Drama Services, said yes: "If the royalty has been paid, then no problem."

Seven publishers said no. However, all would provide or consider special arrangements. Baker's said it would "happily extend rental time frames and adjust to specific needs of a producer/director. An in-advance request in writing from a producing organization will be carefully considered." Likewise, MTI will "always provide the score ahead of time, at no extra rental charge, when the performance license has been received." And Eldridge invites customers "to contact us for early release of scripts and scores. Many times we ship books in the summer with bills dated for September."

Samuel French noted that "Most rental periods can be extended to fit individual requirements and all there needs to be done is to speak to the head of the appropriate licensing department. There could be an additional charge, depending on the length of time and/or other circumstances."

Two companies (Pioneer and Clark) do not rent. Said Pioneer: "They are available for purchase only, which our customers strongly prefer. All our prices are very competitive with rental fees, yet allow directors the freedom to purchase materials as they need them, rather than according to our schedule."

> SCENARIO THREE: *A director is considering one of your plays. She is unsure, however, if she can cast it. At auditions, she provides the actors with photocopied pages of selected scenes. If she can cast the show successfully, she will order scripts for everyone.*

Score: Yes: 2   No: 5   Maybe: 3

As the score sheet indicates, this is a gray area. Two companies—Contemporary Drama Services and Pioneer Drama Service—said yes to this scenario. Pioneer said the practice is acceptable "as long as *all* photocopies are destroyed immediately after casting the show, and each and every actor has an original script from which to work."

Five publishers said absolutely not. Baker's Plays: "It is illegal, it sets a bad example, one that may be imitated and limits the financial gains due the author (book royalty)." Eldridge noted that "Most actors need time to study and enrich their roles. Buy several scripts in advance of auditions and let the actors have time to check them out." MTI said that "for auditions, we can provide perusal material (usually one or two copies of the full show) prior to the shipment of the full set of books."

Three said they might consider such a request. Encore: "[We may] authorize you to go ahead, provided that copies will be destroyed after use." Anchorage said it might grant a request for "a single page or two at most, but not to copy every page and pass out." Likewise, I.E. Clark: "We always try to accommodate our customers. If she will explain her situation, we will consider giving permission to copy a few pages. But she must not copy any part of a play without permission."

SCENARIO FOUR: *An instructor provides students with photocopies of selected scenes from one of your plays for classroom use (no performance).*

Score: Yes: 0   No: 5   Maybe: 5

The doctrine of fair use is clearly open to interpretation. Five companies voiced a flat no, citing ethical as well as legal concerns. Said Samuel French: "Federal copyright laws protect the rights of an author as the owner of the material. What better place to demonstrate the respect for the rights of others, and acknowledgment of laws that govern, than in our educational institutions?" Baker's agreed with this assessment: "One communicates [to students] through such behavior that an author's work is valuable as an educational tool, but not worth the book royalties due for the privilege of its use. How is this reasoning fair?"

Eldridge points out that "Our material is still being used, even though it is not on a traditional stage. Rather than photocopy, buy more scripts or use resource books especially designed for classroom work." MTI "can provide the required number of scripts under the terms and conditions of our 'classroom license.' The fee for the rental of these books is usually at a greatly reduced rate."

Five companies said that classroom use might be permissible under certain circumstances, and some of their statements conflict with the previous statements. Encore, for example, said "Providing you own a copy of the playbook, this is legal educational use."

Said Pioneer: "Though this is not an infringement of copyright laws, it is strongly preferable for students to see that the individual scenes are part of an entire play, which they should have the opportunity to read, if they desire. Since royalties are not charged for classroom use, the nominal cost of a classroom set of scripts is more than offset by the fact that the scripts can be used for many years." And Contemporary Drama Service pointed out that many of its books of scripts give permission to photocopy. "If there is no permission given, we prefer that you check with us first. We evaluate on a case-by-case basis."

SCENARIO FIVE: *The script offered by your company is available for rental only. A company receives the rental materials from you, but needs extra copies of the script for the stage manager, assistant to the director, light-board operator, prop person, etc. Since blocking and cues will be written (and rewritten) on these, photocopies are made, three-hole-punched, and put into binders.*

Score: Yes: 0   No: 2   Maybe: 2   Not Applicable: 6

Six of the companies (Anchorage, Broadway, Clark, Contemporary Drama Services, Eldridge, and Pioneer) do not rent materials. Of the four that do, two said this scenario was unacceptable. "We can provide additional copies to the standard package at a small additional rental fee," MTI said. And Samuel French suggested that because almost all its plays and musicals have the acting edition and/or libretti for sale, "One of our scripts may be pasted into a binder and used as a stage manager's book."

Two publishers said maybe. "Requesting an exception to the norm well in advance in writing under these circumstances will assure our careful consideration," Baker's said. "But photocopies under no circumstances should be made without permission, and the publisher/agent's decision, under the law, must be respected." Likewise, Encore: "Call or write first and obtain permission. If the scripts are destroyed or returned to the publisher for destruction afterwards, it may be all right."

More Thoughts

We invited our respondents to share any additional thoughts on the subject of photocopies.

"If permission to photocopy is not expressly granted in the copyright statement," said Contemporary, "we prefer you check with us first." We think this is a good general rule of thumb with any publisher.

"Our responses may make us appear rapacious—no, Virginia, Scrooge was not a drama publisher—but unfortunately, our materials are easily stolen," explained Eldridge. "Because we serve a large school drama market, we are especially sensitive to photocopies being handed out to students. Those illegal copies give the unspoken message that theft is acceptable. We feel that too many people already are unaware of this important law."

"With express-delivery services, materials can reach you quickly," was the comment of Encore. "Oftentimes it is cheaper to buy legal copies from the publisher than make illegal ones."

"We urge producers to tell us their problems," said Clark. "We always help if we can." MTI, too, said it would work with a theater company or school to resolve any of the scenarios we presented.

Several publishers made strong statements that we think underscore the *real* reason for copyright and contractual constraints.

"The theater's existence depends on the written word," said Baker's. "Playwrights attempt to earn a living from the writing of that written word. Illegal use of the playwright's work steals from his capacity to earn a livelihood. There are no 'gray areas' regarding photocopying. The law is the law, and 'no' means 'no.' "

Echoing this was Samuel French's statement that "It is only reasonable that an author be compensated for his/her efforts in creating the play or scene under consideration. . . . To photocopy all or part of a play is to deprive an author of the money he or she would otherwise earn from the sale of the published acting edition of the play."

Pioneer Drama Service agreed: "We try to provide excellent customer service, but we must also represent our playwrights as best we can and protect the rights of their materials. It is only by doing this that we can continue to attract quality writers to publish their plays with us."

"Generally, publishers of plays print such small quantities that script sales are break-even or at a loss," said Broadway Play. "Photocopying undermines this even more. If people want us to publish plays, they have to support us."

This point, it seems to us, is too often overlooked. Aside from the legal and ethical issues presented here, there is the matter of supporting those whose creativity feeds our own.

FIRST STEPS

*P*lanning the production and your approach to it is extremely important. If you think that a good-looking production is as easy as using the best creative people, you're only half right. There's another factor as well—the "you" factor. As director, you are the important link in the success of those who will help you put this production together.

This section discusses the type of work that needs to be done before rehearsals begin and through that early period—with the notable exception of auditions, which are covered fully in *The Stage Directions Guide to Auditions*.

8 | *Getting It All Together*
How to Work with Your Production Team

Scenic designer, costume designer, lighting designer—all sometimes speak of "directorial sabotage." This happens when designers feel they've done everything possible to create strong visuals, only to be done in by the director.

How can you avoid sabotaging what is, after all, so important to you? Start by being aware of your tremendous influence on the overall success of the creative process. Then consider these seven tips.

1. *Choose well.* When you work with a designer for the first time, take a careful look at the work samples he or she shows you. Yes, chemistry is important, but so is the designer's philosophy, style, and method of working. If you're not completely comfortable with that, you won't be happy with the product they produce for you. Don't work with a designer with whom you've worked before and had problems unless you have a chance to talk about your differences. If you haven't resolved your issues, they'll be right back to haunt you again.

2. *Make sure your expectations are realistic.* You may want your next production to look something like the Broadway

original, but are you being reasonable? Can you afford it? Can your staff build it? Can your theater hold it?

3. *Be prepared.* Show your designers examples of what you like and what you don't like, what has worked for you in the past and what hasn't worked for you. Clip ideas from books and magazines that strike your fancy. Make it clear you're not expecting designers to copy these ideas slavishly, but rather use them as a shortcut to explaining your vision of the look you want.

4. *Explain your vision.* Give designers a firm idea of what you see in your mind's eye. Give them creative room, but give them direction. (You are the director, aren't you?) Nothing is more frustrating to a designer than "Oh, I don't know, just come up with something and I'll let you know what I think," and then, after hours of hard work, to be told, "That's not what I had in mind."

5. *Give praise when it's due and criticize constructively.* It's easy to tell people you don't like something. If you find a designer going in the right direction, say so, even if it's not entirely what you want: "Oh, Rachel, those are wonderful colors for the ensemble. I think you've created a beautiful stage picture. Do you think we could have Jack Point in something brighter so he'll stand out from them?"

6. *Remember this is a collaborative process.* Make sure your designers work with each other as well as they do with you. Beautiful sets and costumes are worthless without appropriate lighting. And vice versa. You want all aspects of a show to be part of a unified whole.

7. *Respect their time.* The creative process takes many hours. It's difficult to design well under extreme pressure. If you want high-quality results, give designers enough time to do it. Start working with them as early as possible, even if it's just throwing out ideas. Most designers do a great deal of visualizing long before they commit anything to paper (or computer screen).

Working with the First-Time Designer

"What bothers me is that nothing in this final drawing is *my* idea." The speaker was the scenic designer of a community-theater production. This was his first time out as designer, although he had proven to be creative and talented as a set artist in earlier productions. At the close of this, their third meeting, the director felt good about the progress of planning sessions and said he hoped the designer shared this enthusiasm. Then the bomb fell.

The director wasn't sure what to say. There was a strained moment of silence. Then the designer added: "I guess I feel dishonest about my name being on the program as scenic designer, because I didn't really design it." So *that* was it.

"I realized at that moment my first-time designer didn't really understand the collaborative process," the director says. "I think he was under the impression that it was his job to come up with the ideas, and it was my job to pick the best one." And he *had* come up with dozens of ideas.

"They were original, often daring, always imaginative," explains the director. "But I've worked on this particular stage for almost twenty years and I knew they wouldn't work. At our first meeting, he came in with an armload of sketches. I praised his creativity, then explained the realities of the stage, the sight lines, and the demands of the script.

"Gradually, over three meetings, our discussions generated a lot of good ideas. Frankly, I wasn't keeping score about whose had survived. We brought in the costume and lighting designers, and of course their suggestions got worked in as well." So now here they were, at a point when the director felt the set was beginning to take final shape. The designer, however, was having misgivings.

"I told him we still didn't have a design. What we had was a concept. For a moment, he thought I was playing semantic games. But I explained that I needed him to take our somewhat fragile idea and turn it into a workable three-dimensional space where I could place and move my actors. We weren't home yet; we had just found the right road. He finally understood."

The moral, suggests this director, is that when working with a first-time designer—whether it be sets, costumes, or lighting—make sure he or she understands that the preliminary work will be of necessity a collaborative effort.

"Also, make sure he understands the theater space you've got. You may need to summarize the positives and negatives. Make time for brainstorming—and for occasional reality checks. Otherwise, it's too easy to get swept up in the creative process and forget your responsibility to the show. I think it's the responsibility of the designer to provide visual and spacial coherence. But the director has to think of much more. After all, you and your actors will be living on this set for a lot of hours of rehearsal and performance."

Off to a Good Start 9

Set the Ground Rules Early—and Stick to Them

As is so often the case, an ounce of prevention is worth a pound of cure. Many problems that arise during rehearsal could be avoided by letting everyone know at the outset what is expected of them. And perhaps more than anything else, that is the director's job—communicating those expectations.

While rules can be stated verbally, it's better (and more official) if every actor is given a sheet of paper with a few basic rules. While you may have additional comments or suggestions, the following rules make a good basis for such a sheet. This is what you want from your cast and crew.

1. Come to rehearsal prepared to work—physically, mentally, and emotionally.

2. Bring a script and pencil.

3. Be prompt. If you know you will be late or must miss a rehearsal, contact me or the assistant director.

4. When I have stopped the proceedings to fix a line or piece of business, begin by repeating the cue line or lines just before the one corrected so the change can be rehearsed.

5. Share scenes rather than steal them. Remember you always look better with a strong partner. Never upstage another actor unless so directed.

6. Don't move, gesture, or face out front on another actor's line unless so directed.

7. Counter-cross and dress the stage without being told.

8. Stay in character. Never talk under your breath or attempt to break up another actor.

9. If you forget a line, remain in character and request "Line."

10. Never give direction to another actor. If you feel a scene could be improved by a change, talk to me.

11. If I give you movement or change a direction, don't argue. If you have a question, wait until after rehearsal or until the next one.

12. Learn your lines precisely and give cues consistently.

13. If you bring in food or drink to rehearsal, clean up after yourself. Do not bring food or drink onto the stage unless they are props.

14. Protect your health, particularly if overtired.

15. Acknowledge fellow actors and production staff when you feel they have done a good job or gone out of their way for you. Remember that you're not the only one who needs positive reinforcement.

16. Don't gossip or spread stories about other cast members, the director, or anyone else in the show. Focus on creating an ensemble. Good productions demand teamwork; consider everyone as part of your team.

Great Expectations

10

Here's how several different directors set down those rules from the beginning, which means from the first rehearsal.

A Successful Opening Night Begins with the First Rehearsal

NANCIANNE PFISTER

I f there's to be magic on opening night, the most logical starting place for creating that magic is the first meeting of the cast. We asked four directors how they handle this all-important first cast gathering.

Working methods vary, but all agreed the first rehearsal is the time to set the ground rules, letting cast members know exactly what will be expected of them. Young actors, who may never have been in a show, may especially need to have these expectations clearly established. So will anyone who has never worked for this particular company or director.

"I have a whole orientation meeting," says James Carver, formerly of Michigan's Kalamazoo Civic Players. "I describe the process. I tell them what they can expect from me and what I expect from them."

Carver uses the first meeting to dispel the myth that acting is just a matter of knowing your lines and not bumping into the furniture.

"I tell the cast that I expect their promptness and their creativity. I expect them to study, to do most of their work away from rehearsal. I expect to see evidence that they have thought about the show and about their character. I expect the cast to know—or learn quickly—basic stage directions. I expect them to keep notebooks and to study the characters, not just the lines."

The role of the director in all this?

"I am the chief interpreter of the script," Carver insists. "I am responsible for a cohesive picture, so it's important that actors don't direct other actors."

We were not surprised to hear this last statement from every director with whom we spoke.

Learning the Ropes

Carver knows novice actors may need something extra and they can expect him to supply it. He may have to explain a method of study or demonstrate how to analyze a script, reading for the subtext.

Almost all cast members in Margaret McClatchy's shows are novices. McClatchy is director at Shawnee Mission High School outside Kansas City. She does not do a readthrough at the first cast meeting, but rather uses the time to set the atmosphere she hopes to maintain during the rehearsal period.

"Congratulations!" she tells her cast. "You are my first choice. You know how many people auditioned, but I chose *you*. The law of averages says you won't all make it to opening night. Here is what we all have to do to get there."

With that introduction, McClatchy discusses "everything that will happen from now until strike. I explain how to read a script, how to highlight your lines."

Reinforcing the idea of teamwork, she discusses the schedule of evening and Saturday rehearsals, reminding students that missing a rehearsal can jeopardize the show.

"The acceptable conflicts were listed on the audition form. If there are others, they have to say so. They saw the crowd at auditions; they know they can be replaced. And I have done so."

McClatchy also talks about things that can jeopardize more than the show.

"Each student signs a form pledging to neither use nor possess drugs and alcohol. This form is then signed by parents and returned."

It's a Circus

Diane Crews claims her first readthrough is "like a three-ring circus. Everyone comes. Not just cast members but their parents, too. We give them a huge packet of information and I try to say as much as I can while they are all here."

Crews, founder and artistic director of Dreamwrights Youth & Family Theatre in York, Pennsylvania, talks about being on time for rehearsal, explaining that call time is start time, so it's wise to arrive ten minutes early.

"Our kids must be picked up on time. This is not a day-care center."

Most of the expectations Crews discusses involve a child's taking responsibility so his or her actions do not interfere with the rehearsal process. Children are told, "You are responsible for yourself, for your stuff, your trash, your entrance, your lines, your props, your schedule—no fair saying your mom didn't know you had a rehearsal."

While his casts are composed mostly of adults, Ron Hannemann of Vive Les Arts in Killeen, Texas, also writes out his expectations on a handout for distribution during the first cast meeting. Like Carver, McClatchy, and Crews, he begins by explaining the basic courtesy of arriving fifteen minutes early for rehearsal. He adds that the actor must arrive sober. Hannemann insists that rehearsal time not be polluted by other concerns.

"While we are in rehearsal, that time is mine. If there's a break, I expect people to be making notes or running lines. Save the other conversation for your own time."

He also insists on preparation before rehearsal.

"I expect cast members to do their homework. If they read the script and there's an occupation they don't know about, I expect them to go to the library and find out."

Hannemann allows cast members to make suggestions, but tells them to keep in mind they are just that: suggestions. He also admits that at some first-time cast meetings, he's had a rude awakening.

"Sometimes I cast someone whom I suddenly know is all wrong, either by size or attitude or interpretation. And some people have wonderful auditions but never get any better. I have the vision; I have to make it work."

It's clear from these four directors that it's a hazardous trip from auditions to opening night. To arrive safely, each performer must know what is expected and deliver it.

"It amazes me," says James Carver. "We open the doors at auditions and cast ten strangers. Twenty-five rehearsals later, we have an ensemble."

It must be the magic.

11 | *Make Time Work for You*

A director is responsible for so many different aspects of a production that balancing all the different demands on your time is perhaps your most difficult challenge. And that challenge is greatest in the weeks leading up to the opening.

How to Keep on Top of Things Throughout the Rehearsal Period

No matter how many rehearsals you've scheduled, you always end up feeling you need another week. At least that's the feeling of most directors we know. There are no two ways about it: Time is the most valuable item on your budget. Used badly, it becomes your worst enemy.

You will never have too much time. Whatever production schedule you work out, examine it carefully and realistically. Relate the number of working sessions to the ground you've got to cover, and plan everything out beforehand. If you can control the time factor, you have a better chance for a successful production.

First, don't try to cram too much into any one rehearsal. Inevitably, some unforeseen aspect will take up much more time than you thought, and you may find you have to reschedule what's left to another session. But what will be bumped if you do? Or will you have to add a rehearsal period—and when? So, it makes sense to give yourself some wiggle room at each rehearsal. If you end up letting people go home early, that's all right. They'll thank you, and perhaps be more rested for the next rehearsal.

Second, try to schedule more rehearsal sessions than you actually think you'll need; if you don't need them, you can give the cast a night off and boost morale. Far better to do that than ask the cast to come in for an extra rehearsal at the last moment—assuming they are even available.

You can build a security cushion by putting "TBA" or "clean-up and fix" rehearsals on the schedule from the start. You'll find these especially useful after the first runthrough of an act or of the entire show. During the runthrough, make notes of what needs work and then fix them in the TBA session. If you try to fix things during a runthrough, even of an act, you hold up others and slow down the gelling process.

Consider scheduling at least one clean-up session the week before opening, particularly if the show is a musical or large-cast effort. At this point you should be on stage, with some semblance of a set, and can spend even a few hours profitably by fixing what doesn't look or work right. Warning: Avoid major changes at this point—this is a cleanup, not a reconstruction.

Finally, remember what can be accomplished in any one rehearsal depends on the size and experience of the cast, their fatigue level, the difficulty of the material, and the creativity and energy you can provide as director.

12 | *Off Book, On Target*

Offstage Readers During Rehearsal Get Actors Out of the Script and Into the Play

SUE WURSTER

*I*t was clear during auditions this young man was something special. It wasn't just that he was obviously ambitious and responsible—after all, he had memorized three scenes for the tryouts. No, there was something else there as well. He had a gift. No one was surprised to see his name at the top of the cast list that week—despite the fact he was new to the school and a freshman to boot. The surprise came when he arrived in my classroom to pick up his book.

"I have to tell you something," he said shyly. "I memorized those scenes because I can't read. What I mean is, it's really hard for me, and I can't read and act at the same time. Don't worry—I learn my lines really fast. But maybe you can help me? My teacher in my old school used to have somebody read my lines for me in rehearsals. I'd just repeat them. I'm an auditory learner."

I couldn't get what he had said out of my mind. And the more I thought about it, the more sense it made to me. No one can read and act at the same time. I decided to take a chance and try something radically different with that show, *The Diviners*, by Jim Leonard—something I think works with young or older actors, high school students, or actors of long experience.

First, I dispensed with the traditional initial full-cast readthrough. It had never struck me as a particularly valuable exercise anyway—for the most part, actors frequently pay little attention whenever their characters are not speaking or being addressed. Instead, we talked about the world of the play and improvised the moments of the piece actually creating the spine of the script, onstage, at the very outset.

We worked encounter by encounter throughout the whole play, making a sort of time line for those encounters and events, and then improvised each, in order. In a way, we created an abridged but accurate version of the play at the very first rehearsal.

We did the entire play—or rather a thirty-minute version of it—that day. Moving directly from one encounter to the next, we really experienced the play's momentum and power. "It was like this huge downpour—like we all nearly drowned," said one cast member.

It was the most electric opening rehearsal I ever had experienced. We hadn't sat around a table for an intellectual classroom exercise—we actually had internalized a production concept by embodying it.

The next step was the most bold and risky. I decided not to single out that auditory learner by giving him an offstage reader—I used my stage manager as *everybody's* offstage reader. No one would carry the script around on stage.

So when the group assembled, we improvised through the scene to be worked. Then we sat on the floor and read through it. We talked and then read through it again. Next, we took about fifteen minutes for the cast members to spread out around the theater and familiarize themselves with the scene. Then we began the staging.

The stage manager sat at the edge of the stage and read the lines of the play. She announced the character and then read his or her line, a natural phrase at a time (without interpretative inflection). The actor simply took in the words and, when ready, repeated that phrase—in action. The reader simply became an auditory script. I provided stage direction along the way.

Initially, it was hard for many of the actors to avoid looking at the reader rather than at the others on stage with them. But this was really no different than when they had buried their faces in the script (as I often had found myself doing as well). It did not take long for all of us to adjust, however, and it soon became a very natural process. The difference in the quality of work was stunning.

How so? For starters, after that first work session on the scene, the play was truly staged. Characters functioned in relation to each other because the actors had been looking at each other from the outset. They were physically engaged in full stage business because they hadn't been trying to juggle scripts when setting it in the first place. They knew the scene—truly "by heart"—because language and action had been linked for them from the outset.

A World of Difference

In the past, readthroughs never had felt particularly valuable, and blocking sessions always had struck me as having been rather aptly named. Everybody walked around with books and pencils in hand that blocked their views of anything and anyone around them as they wrote down directions to be memorized along with lines—later. The right hand truly did not know what the left was doing.

What I call the "treading" sessions usually had come next. Everybody rhythmically moved arms and legs to keep their heads above water, but nobody really got anywhere. Then there were line deadlines, when at least one member of the cast hadn't done all the homework and was winging it, which, of course, just bogged everyone down.

Finally, it seemed to me that rehearsals never really had begun until everyone was finally off book—at best, halfway through the entire process. Working off book from the beginning simply means rehearsals happen from that point as well.

For me, the process has changed dramatically. I now start each show with a "grounding" session in which we focus on the world of the play—its time and/or place, setting, situation—and improvise the key structural moments of the piece. This is followed by staging sessions in which we work on one ten- to fifteen-minute scene at a time. Each session involves talking about the scene, improvising it, sitting down and reading it, talking more fully about it, and reading it again.

We then take a "study break" of about fifteen minutes, in which the actors spread out and individually familiarize themselves with the lines and action of the scene. We then move to staging it. The reader(s) takes hold of the script, and the actors take hold of the stage. By the end of that rehearsal, a good bit of that scene already will be memorized.

Everybody Benefits

I've been using this method for several years now and have found it to be efficient and effective. I like having three rehearsals (two and a half hours each) per week, and I like to do two scenes (or fifteen-minute segments) each week. We spend one day on each scene and then run both at the third rehearsal. At an act break, we usually spend the week running the act before moving on to the next.

I spend about three weeks on each act and then have two weeks of full-run tech/dress rehearsals. Eight weeks—three rehearsals per week. That's it.

We adapt as appropriate to each show or each group, of course. On more shows than not, for example, we use multiple readers— each character having his or her own. I think it is best to keep that character/reader combination a consistent one rather than switching readers around all the time. This means everybody is involved. Techies are truly connected from the beginning and each merely moves away from reading and on to lighting, for example, when his or her character is memorized.

There are marvelous benefits to this. Last year, when we performed *Anansi! A Spider's Tales*, three cast members were absent on the day of our performance. Before I had time to think about panicking, David stepped up to volunteer his services. "I was Natalie's reader anyway—I know it," he said. He did know it. In fact, all three of those cast members' readers knew those roles and stepped in with ease.

In addition to the practical benefits to be accrued from working this way, there are also some more profound lessons I have learned along the way. I find I have become much more aware of the different learning styles my actors use, and I have made more effort to address this. I have seen actors themselves become more aware of the nature of their own styles—"I really can't take in more than about three or four words at a time," one will coach his reader—while another is asking hers to "give me the whole sentence first and then go back to the beginning of it and give me a phrase at a time."

I also have seen my actors become more responsible for their own learning. When an actor connects with a reader, a new element creeps into the process. I have seen many cast members pull their readers aside before the end-of-week run begins. Snatches of "Look—I know this and this and this, but I'm pretty shaky here and here—and I don't know the monologue at all" can be heard about the room. Readers focus and nod.

When it's time to run that sequence again two weeks later, the readers tend to admonish, "Okay . . . but I really have to get to the board, so you better get this down." Actors no longer memorize for a director—they are memorizing for each other or, more importantly, for themselves. It works.

Most of my actors generally learn lines more quickly when

working off book. They are not simply reading from a page, but rather are actively working with language that seems to help spark the engine, so to speak.

But there are still actors who have difficulty with memorization. With the reader method, your production is always progressing at the pace of the quickest rather than the slowest members of the group, which is exciting for most—but which can be a bit frightening for the slower. I recognize those actors more quickly than I did in the past. It becomes apparent at the end of the first week, when running what we've done. Most will be virtually off book and reader—but a few still will be heavily dependent. It's usually fairly apparent when the difficulty involves more than a time-management problem.

Because that potential problem is apparent early on, I can step in more quickly than in the past. As a result, those actors get help more quickly and avoid a great deal of potential embarrassment later in the process.

With the reader method, I feel as though I am working more collaboratively with my students. Ensemble seems to develop more quickly. There is much less temperament connected to the whole process, which means there is far less stress involved. For me, directing off book really has resulted in on-target production.

STAGING THE PLAY

PART

III

Much of the director's job is facetiously dubbed "traffic control." There's a grain of truth here. Ensuring a smooth flow of movement, grouping actors effectively, helping the audience focus on what is important—all these *are* part of your responsibility. But there is far more thought and creativity involved than merely pointing the way.

Here are some insights into the ways in which you can approach the staging of a production.

13 | Using the Framing Device
Here's How to Bring the Action Full Circle

*H*ave you noticed how often a good novel, play, or film returns us to the place where it began—albeit with new knowledge on the part of the characters? Indeed, writers often emphasize the degree of character growth (or decline) by returning them to a setting similar to the opening. In *Oedipus the King*, Oedipus is first seen walking majestically out of the royal palace of Thebes, totally in control. At play's end, the blinded king is led out by an attendant.

Chekhov carefully sets the last act of *The Cherry Orchard* in the same room we first see in May, when the cherry trees were in flower, but which now gives off a sense of desolation. There are no longer any curtains on the windows or pictures on the walls. What little furniture there is left is piled up in a corner as if for sale.

Arthur Miller's *The Crucible* begins in a bedroom in which "the morning sunlight streams" through a leaded glass window; it ends with the death of John Proctor, while his wife listens to the drum roll, "the new sun . . . pouring in upon her face."

These are examples of one sort of framing device—perhaps the most commonly used. Sometimes the frame is blatantly obvious—for example, *Sunday in the Park with George* with its "blank canvas." In other cases it is more subtle, as with the onstage narrator who opens and closes *The Glass Menagerie* or *Dancing at Lughnasa.*

Some plays have framing devices as part of the plot. In *The Beggar's Opera*, for example, the Beggar starts the action, then steps in to halt the proceedings before Macheath is executed. *The Taming of the Shrew* has half of a frame (the Christopher Sly scene); the other half seems to have disappeared, perhaps conveniently forgotten by the Bard.

The frame need not be the return of a setting or a particular character. In some plays, it might be a word or phrase from the opening or one that sums up the story. Consider the last line of *The Importance of Being Earnest*, for example, or the mother's litany against knives in the first minute of *Blood Wedding*, which at play's end returns as a solemn reminder of the tragedy that has just occurred.

As a director, you should be on the lookout for frames. If the author has indicated an obvious one, don't hide it. Point it up. On the other hand, if the author has not provided such a device, see if you can add one. This can be especially useful in those plays that seem to leave the audience up in the air, although most plays can benefit from a sense of coming full circle.

For example, in a production of *Inherit the Wind,* a director took advantage of the town-square setting that opens and closes the show. In the opening scene, the townspeople put up a banner that says "READ YOUR BIBLE." At play's end, as everyone leaves the square, he allowed there to be a moment of quiet, then dimmed the lights, leaving one spot on this banner, which by this time had come loose at one end, hanging sadly in the wind.

She Loves Me is a musical that relates how two strong-headed people fall in love through a lonely hearts club—despite all the obstacles they strew in their own paths. To frame the show, a director had the curtain open as the audience was seated. Viewers saw a street and a lamppost on which a mailbox was attached. Light from the street lamp (and a subdued spotlight) highlighted the mailbox. At show's end, the two lovers kiss and walk off, the woman pausing only to kiss her palm and then touch the mailbox. The lights then dimmed, leaving only the lamppost and mailbox visible; fadeout.

As you can see, frames can be a powerful device for bringing closure to a play, for reassuring the audience that loose ends have been tied up. Not all plays benefit from the framing technique, and it can be done with too heavy a hand or used too often. However, used carefully and in sympathy with the playwright's intentions, the frame can be one of the most useful tools at the director's disposal.

14 | *The Case for Delayed Blocking*

Questions about blocking? In this and the next few chapters, you'll find some solutions to help solve your blocking problems.

Sometimes a Different Approach Can Be Useful

MICHAEL KANTER

O n the stage, action is drama, for without appropriate action to animate the scenes, the play becomes static, uneventful, dramatically dull.

Blocking—setting the movement of actors on stage and composing the pictures of the play—too often gets out of hand, becoming a fetish in the hands of directors who insist on blocking the play just a few days into rehearsal, or even the first day for a stock production allowed only one week of rehearsal.

While many directors like to jump in and set stage movement almost immediately, I find getting the actors up on their feet is desirable only after they have become familiar enough with the sound and continuity of the dialogue and feel free to move in synchronization with the dialogue. With the script in hand, most actors are awkward in movement. I much prefer to have them get a firm grip on the style and techniques of dialogue, interacting with the other actors, before preoccupying themselves with movement, even the most tentative blocking.

With a melodrama, or any play depicting violence or dependent on stage action or needing careful, artful composition of many characters on stage, blocking does indeed become vital. However, most plays do not fall into these categories.

Before attempting any blocking, I prefer to get the sense of the actors' presence and strength of delivery. I let them read through scenes several times, on their feet, but without specific blocking from me. I want to see the actor move in rehearsal. Is he physically deft or clumsy? Can she keep her movement free from the rhythm of the dialogue? Can he achieve a smooth blending of voice and action so the performance does not become mechanical? (Many actors are most effective when they do *not* move.) To what extent can the power of the scene be left almost entirely to delivery, without introducing extraneous movement? Too often, the director begins by blocking actors without really knowing them, without understanding their strengths and weaknesses, or what they can bring to the part at hand.

I distrust the wisdom of the director who immediately says to his cast, "Tomorrow we will block the show." Sometimes it is better first to watch and listen.

15 | *When to Block out of Sequence*

Flexibility Sometimes Is More Important Than Strict Order

Many directors block in strict scene order, from Act I, Scene 1, to the end of the play. But there can be problems with this method. Because characters often come and go throughout the play, the actors will have to come back on successive nights, even if for only a few minutes of blocking each time. Instead, you might consider blocking groups of scenes that use the same actors. That way, you'll lessen the problem of people coming night after night for only a few lines. You don't even have to block whole scenes, if it helps you group people more efficiently. This is what is known as "French scenes."

French scenes are not marked in a script. Rather, a French scene begins with the entrance of one character and ends with the exit of the same or another character, or with the entrance of a third character. Go through the script, noting the page numbers for each French scene and the names of the characters involved; number each scene in succession. Then create a list showing each character and the French scenes in which they take part.

Of course, the principal characters will appear most often, and frequently alone or with the other principals. The supporting characters appear less frequently and often spread throughout the play, so they will benefit the most from your grouping their scenes together for blocking purposes. But principals benefit as well, because you can zero in on their scenes in depth without worrying that you're keeping others waiting.

A quick way to put together a blocking schedule is to list and number each French scene and list the characters who take part in each one. Next, list each character and after their name write the numbers of the scenes in which they appear (for example, "George 1, 3, 6, 12, 14"). Then match characters who appear in scenes together. Hand out the list of French scenes listed by character and a schedule showing which scenes will be blocked each night ("Monday: 3, 5, 7, 18"). To find out if they have been called, actors need only look to see if the numbers match those on their character sheet. Note that this method is for blocking purposes and early rehearsals only. After a few weeks, you will want to develop the continuity that only straight runthroughs can provide.

16 | Ahead of the Crowd

How to Handle Large Groups on Stage

Some plays—and most musicals—call for a large group onstage at some point. Indeed, you may have picked a show precisely because it gives a large number of people a chance to be on stage.

However, as a director, you may find you haven't enough time to spend in developing characterization for each member of the ensemble. One approach is to use an assistant director to work with these people, someone who understands your vision for the production and can translate this for members of the group.

Asking each member of the crowd to develop his or her own character is risky unless the actors are experienced. A better way is to gather the group together, explain the show, the historical period, the essential action, your concept and plan for the show, and how the ensemble fits into this. Then have the ensemble split up into smaller groups of six to eight people. Let the actors within each group discuss their characterization. Let them invent a history for the character, personality quirks, and so on. Make sure each person in the group understands what the others are planning, then have them stand near each other on stage so they can interact appropriately.

For example, if one actor decides to be hard of hearing, another can help by talking into his ear. Stanislavsky once said, "There are no small parts, only small actors." Chorus or ensemble players need to remember that everyone on stage is important and that it takes only one person out of character to ruin a scene.

The surest way to invite ruin is to let a crowd ad lib on stage without some guidance. Remember that the *appearance* of spontaneity is enough. If the play takes place in a historical setting, the actors should know enough not to say "Wow!," for example. Decide what the appropriate ad libs might be and stick with them. Some directors insist that a crowd should murmur something like "rhubarb" when conversing among themselves. The idea is to give the illusion of speech without anything too specific that might distract from the main action.

Members of groups or choruses sometimes must be reminded they are not normally the main object of interest on stage. A director should explain the focus of each scene, and how the group can help the audience focus as well. Often, this means grouping crowds appropriately or minimizing their movement.

In general, keep minor characters around the periphery of the stage whenever possible, encouraging the principal character's moving to direct speeches to them. Put the leading player on a higher level than the crowd when possible, such as on a bench, stairs, or a rock. Or have the crowd sit on the ground or on chairs.

Finally, have an assistant watch for the common failings of actors in crowds on stage, such as anticipating the reaction to a particular line. In their enthusiasm, inexperienced actors often vocalize excitement or disappointment a fraction before the speech that is supposed to motivate them. And remember, most members of the chorus or crowd actually *enjoy* getting notes from the director—it makes them feel important.

Crowd Scenes Made Easy

Instead of blocking each member of the crowd separately, first divide people into groups (such as, Group A, B, or C). Then give one set of entrances and exits: "Group A comes in through the stage left door, Group B down the center rear steps, and Group C from stage right around the rocks."

Next, unless the group is a mob and acting with one mind, assign character and motivation in subgroups. For example, you might want one or two people in each group to be very verbal, another two to use extravagant gestures, some others to be bored with the action, and so on.

In other words, go for the big picture. Once this is established, encourage the actors to add business where appropriate. The advantage here is you save a great deal of time and effort, while also projecting the image of an organized director who knows what he or she wants. And that is worth something all by itself.

Divide and Conquer

Subdividing a stage into discrete playing areas is another good technique for working with large groups of people. Many actors, especially inexperienced ones, find it useful to imagine the stage as a giant tic-tac-toe board, instead of memorizing the upstage/downstage/stage right/stage left configuration.

Communication between director and actor is improved because the director can say, "Elwood walks from 7 to 5, pauses, and moves to the table in 3." If the stage were divided along the lines of the following diagram, this would translate as "Elwood enters upstage right, walks center stage, pauses, and then moves to the table downstage left."

7	8	9
4	5	6
1	2	3

Such a setup also helps your lighting designer. With the acting areas divided into sections, the lighting of each area can be carefully controlled. It also allows for continuity, so an actor can move from area to area and remain well lighted.

Areas should not be too small or they become difficult to light and their location confusing to the actors. On the other hand, if the areas are too large, lighting them well may be difficult, and again their boundaries won't be clear. If our diagram is of a stage area 24 feet by 24 feet, each of the nine sections would each be eight feet square. This is about right for both acting and lighting purposes.

ACTOR AND DIRECTOR

*E*very director works out his or her own method of working with actors. It may derive from training, experience, or basic personality traits, but if successful, it can be added to the storehouse of directing knowledge.

We have talked with a number of directors about their methods and found a remarkable similarity of philosophy. All agreed that while they have a preferred method, it's best to be flexible, using different approaches for different plays, scenes, and actors. In this section, we look at some of those approaches.

17 | A Matter of Style
How You Direct Depends on the Play and the Actors

W hile some directors are naturally open or collaborative or highly structured, it's our experience that the best are a combination.

Probably the most common approach is to discuss interpretation with the actor, making sure he or she understands the inner workings of the scene. "A lot of problems are the result of a lack of understanding of what actors need to express," says one director. "You have to help the actor live within the fictional circumstances and help him understand the full implication of the scene in terms of his character," says another.

A director also can use questions and discussions to bring out the actor's own interpretation of a scene. If the actor's interpretation is markedly different from your own, you need to use some pointed questions, such as "How do you account for your character's actions at the start of Act Two?" or "What does Jane want in her life and in each scene in the play?" While these encourage the actors to take charge of their characters, you are the one pointing the way. Your questions can help them understand your vision of the play as well.

Suggest ways in which the actor can find the characterization or emotion he seeks. This is a highly individual matter, of course, because some actors are more adept than others at using memory or free association to help them along the way. One approach is to relate the emotions of the character to the actor's own experience: "Remember, Don, when you lost your mother? That's the kind of feeling you need to bring to your character in Scene Five." However, you need to know your actors very well in order to guide them in this way.

Make sure the actor understands the way scenes are constructed, where the high points are, and how the play moves to a logical conclusion so the characterization is in synch with the rest the show.

It's also important to make sure the actors understand *your* vision so they can work out their own responses to it. "If the actors don't understand what you see or hear in your head," says one director, "they certainly aren't going to be able to give you what you want."

The actor's scenes give only a portion of the character's life. After all, the characters exist before they are introduced, and have a life off stage while the play is going on. Some directors use improvisations or discussions to help actors create this other life—for example, details of a prior relationship or an event that takes place just before the play begins. As rehearsals began for a production of *A Little Night Music*, the actress playing Desiree wrote a letter in character to the three characters to whom she was closest—her mother, her daughter, her lover—and shared them with the actors playing those roles.

Another collaborative approach is to stop the actor at key points in the scene and ask, "Why did your character say that just now?" or "What's running through her mind when she hears the phone ring?" or "What does your character *really* want from her friend here?" This may work best after the scene is blocked and the actors are beginning to work on delivery and characterization.

In Shakespearean or other classic plays, the language may be a problem for the actors. In such cases, some directors ask the actors to rephrase the lines in their own words. Once a scene is run in this manner, the actors return to the original words and run it again. This accomplishes several things. First, it indicates whether the actor actually understands the meaning intended by the author. Second, it helps the actor shade the delivery to emphasize that meaning. And, third, it may reveal a nuance or interpretation that can be used by the other actors in the scene. It's also possible you might garner fresh insight yourself.

Even in blocking, you can give actors some leeway by indicating a general concept for the scene and letting them find their own movements within this framework. For example: "I want you to stay close to the window—remember, your wife is coming home at any moment—and as long as you do that, anything else physical you want to try is fine. Keep it comfortable for you."

Finally, let the actor suggest ideas if you suddenly feel stuck. "This cross isn't working, Don. I've got to get you over to Janet. How do *you* think your character would do that?" The directors we talked with agreed that most actors are flattered by the attention and feel good about contributing. "I think it's also good for a director to admit once in a while that he's not God," says one. "Putting a play together is a cooperative effort, anyway, so why not admit it? You can ask for input while still making it clear that suggestions have to work within the context you've established."

A Firmer Hand

Sometimes, however, a director needs to exercise more control of a play. This may be due to the inexperience of one or more of the actors, for example, or because of the demands of the script, or time constraints. Most directors we've heard from say they are not in favor of a strict authoritarian style, however.

"That's not fun for me or the actors," explains one. "It works against the creative force."

But all seem to agree there are ways to give structure while allowing for some creativity on the part of the actors.

"You'll always have a better working relationship with your actors if you allow them to be active participants, even in small ways," notes one director.

Basically, this boils down to providing specific direction on placement, movement, and motivation. This helps the actors understand what you want visually, while giving them the chance to make sense of it in terms of their own abilities.

As you audition and cast a show, make mental or written notes that indicate the type of direction each actor may need. In directing, one style does not fit all. For example:

1. You might suggest that somewhere in a particular speech you want the actor to stand up and cross, then let him find the appropriate place. "Most actors can understand the need for variety of placement and movement," says one director. "They just want to feel comfortable with that movement. Letting them decide the movent may be enough." On the other hand, you may feel the need to be hardnosed about when and how a character moves, or

delivers a line. If you explain it in terms of your vision of the show, you'll usually find that an actor will follow your lead.

2. You can give the actor specific movement and motivation and still leave some room for interpretation. "Dorothy is so upset that she just can't see straight," you might explain. "Turn away from John quickly, then move away, just missing the edge of the table. End up anywhere upstage left you want."

3. A related method is to achieve the effect you want and let the actor try to find a way to do it. "Dorothy is so upset that she can't see straight. She can't stand to be next to John and feels trapped. She needs to get upstage left in time for the phone to ring." You're planting the seed here, but the result will seem to come from the actor, not you.

4. When actors have a difficult time creating a particular emotion or attitude, you may be able to show them how you want them to look or move. But it's not enough to simply move or emote; you need to help them understand the underlying motivation. Few actors can replicate another person's thought or behavior; they can only approximate it, based on their own skill and understanding.

5. Sometimes you need an exact movement or delivery in order for the audience to understand a joke or plot element. Most actors understand when this sort of direction is necessary, so don't apologize for it: "Frankly, Mary, you'll have to emphasize the word *stockings* here, and move quickly to the door, or the audience won't understand you're referring to the clothes hanging on the back of the door."

6. If you must insist on a particular interpretation or movement, demonstrate the mood or feeling or intensity without reading the lines. If you can, improvise something. Make up some lines that have the same dramatic point, and show them how they might be done.

7. As a last resort, tell the actor to do something your way and say, "Trust me." If you've worked hard to instill trust, the actor will follow your lead.

18 | *Play the Intention, Not the Line*

Why the Script Is Only Twenty Percent of a Successful Performance

HE: Good morning.

SHE: Good morning.

HE: Did you sleep well?

The actress pauses and with a facial movement indicates she's not sure she wants to answer his last question. Clearly, something is not quite right between these two, but there is nothing in the lines themselves to indicate this. And that is the point, says Kent Brown, former theater professor at the University of Arkansas, Fayetteville.

"Lines are not what drive a play," he explains. "It's the intent, the subtext, the kernel that's important. Yet, most actors play the line, and that's where they fail."

We heard Brown's views on this subject at a workshop at a national theater conference and were impressed with his approach. Here's what we learned.

Intent, as the dictionary defines it, refers to "a purpose, object, or aim." And, as Brown points out, a character in a play normally has one central objective.

"If the writer's any good, that objective will be fraught with obstacles," he says. "We then watch the character overcome those obstacles. What we call drama lies in the quality of the character's choices as he or she works toward the goal—whether it's achieved or not. As I tell my students, 'No risk, no interest,' and that applies to both drama and comedy: Audiences don't pay to see balance and harmony."

Making a character's intent clear to the audience requires action, Brown reminds us. Indeed, he says, that's what acting *means*. If acting equals action, as he believes, then directing consists largely of helping the actors serve the play by making sure the actions are appropriate, consistent, lifelike, and observable. But a director cannot impose these things on the actor. To be believable, a character must come from within the actor.

"Talk to your actors about their own experiences that relate to those of the characters, but don't overanalyze," he warns. "Actors will ask 'What's my relationship here? How long have we known each other?' Often, we'll talk about this. But sometimes I will just say, 'Let's just see what happens. I might even say, 'Why don't you just do something,' with the emphasis on the *do*. And I will watch and listen as they explore the possibilities."

A working relationship like this is built on mutual trust and clear communication. "As a director, you might tell an actor, 'Ted, why don't you just get that chair and bring it next to her.' If the actor says, 'Where shall I put it?,' he's not really thinking of the character's intention. Instead, he's saying, 'I don't want to be wrong, so tell me how to do it right.' As director, you are moving people on stage, but it's up to the actor to make that move work within his or her character. It's always a matter of choices. There may be a hundred ways to place that chair. Some will work better than others, and each will lead to different choices in the next moment. It's essential that the actor take the lead here, but it's up to the director to make sure the choices being made work for the play as a whole.

"So, don't talk to your people about lines. Don't talk to your people about emotions. If an actor has just delivered the line, 'John—it's great to see you again,' and you say to the actor, 'Paul, you seem flat there. *Give* me something. Pour it on,' Paul is likely to just shout his lines. That's not what you meant, but you didn't help him with the character's intent. Suddenly, Paul feels very vulnerable. He's given you his scream, his tight-veined look, and that's not *right?* He doesn't know what you really want. The crucial trust between actor and director is breaking down."

Instead, Brown suggests, work with the actor. You might suggest, "So, how long has it been since you've *seen* Paul? Are you *glad* to see him or setting him up for the kill?"

"Talk to your actors like intelligent humans and get them to respond in kind," Brown advises, "drawing upon their own life experiences to make the moment work."

Good communication skills can be a director's greatest asset, he believes.

"In rehearsal, when you say, 'Let's take it again,' let them know *why* you're doing it again. For example, you might say, 'There's a kind of stiffness here that's working against the scene' or 'You're playing this as though you already know how the play ends.' "

That latter point can be a serious problem, he believes, because the actors *do* know what's going to happen. And such knowledge can pull them out of the "now." That's why rehearsing line readings is so deadly, he believes. It's mere repetition. But working with *intent* keeps things fresh for the actor, and the result is more real for the audience.

"So, ask difficult questions of your characters, not easy ones," Brown adds. "Ask difficult questions of what the play is about, apart from the story line. In rehearsal, ask if something is missing. Get your cast together the second week of rehearsal and tell them, 'Let's look at Scene One of Act One—are we missing any values there?' And the response should not be, 'Bob isn't loud enough.' A useful response would be, 'I don't think I should be moving away from Jane at this point. I think I have an unresolved problem that would make me want to look at her right in the face.' As director, listen and say, 'Let's try it.' Then *get up there on stage with the actors* and put it under a microscope for a moment."

Brown insists that directors get close to the actors in rehearsal.

"Don't direct from the back of the house. A director must share that space with those actors, especially early on. That's when you see the little movements, the choices being made. There's energy there you can see and work with. Do you have one of those awful table scenes where everyone's seated? Do yourself a favor and sit in a chair alongside the actors and watch what's going on."

If there's an opportunity, a director may want to reblock an act, Brown suggests.

"Reblocking can sometimes give your actors something fresh, give them barriers to overcome, a new view on the situation. It's a great tool when you feel the play isn't coming to life. Actors sometimes rely too much on things—a chair, a movement. They forget the vibrancy of discovery. Changing blocking can add freshness to their performance and life to the play."

Play to the Intelligence

Ultimately, the audience will decide the success of the venture, Brown points out.

"Audiences are more intelligent than we give them credit for," Brown says. "Therefore, in the theater we should play to the most intelligent possibility when we're interpreting a play. Good work is good because it makes the essential human connections. We know how hard it is to do that in our own lives. Don't you think the audience knows it, too? So those on stage need to make it tough, make it real, so the audience can really bond with us in some way and go with us on this incredible journey we call theater."

19 | *Succeeding with Difficult Actors*
Recognizing the Types Is Step One

The problem actor is more than a discipline problem. He saps energy from you and others involved in the production—and energy is something none of us can afford to waste. Problems normally appear the first weeks of rehearsal, and it is then that you must solve or work around them.

A certain amount of tension between director and actor can be a good thing, and there is a fine line between an involved and a difficult actor. That line is crossed when the actor's behavior begins to interfere with the progress of the play. When this happens, you must take decisive action. Otherwise, others involved in the production may come to resent both of you, and you will find yourself with more problems than before.

Difficult actors come in many guises. We've listed a few here, with some ideas on how best to work with them. To avoid the clumsy *he or she,* we've used the pronoun *he* throughout. However, difficult actors—and directors—know no gender lines.

The Cross-Examiner ■ A good director appreciates actors who have thought about their roles and who bring their own point of view to a characterization. But if the actor's questions and suggestions begin to disrupt the rehearsal process, ask him to stay afterward. Tell him plainly that you want him to contribute, but he is interfering with rehearsals and making it difficult for others to concentrate. Ask him to bring questions or suggestions to you *after* each rehearsal. By doing so, you'll not only eliminate the interruptions, you'll also reduce the number of items he will actually remember afterwards. Outside the stress of the rehearsal itself, you may even find some of his ideas make sense. If they do, say so and praise him. If they don't, say you're satisfied with things as they are, at least for the time being.

If, after your chat, he continues to disrupt the rehearsal, stop the proceedings and say, "Don, you agreed to see me after rehearsal if you had questions. Now, let's go on. . . ." This way the cast knows who's in charge.

The Antagonist ■ The Antagonist not only questions your direction in front of others, but also makes jokes or negative comments behind your back. This is truly destructive behavior and must be nipped in the bud. If you find this is typical behavior for this person, get rid of him. *Now*. You don't have the time or energy to fight this battle—and you can't win. If his conduct isn't typical, ask to see him after rehearsal. Tell him that no matter what is going on in his personal life, you won't tolerate disruptiveness. Encourage him to share his feelings with you; you may be able to resolve the behavior problem in the process. However, make it clear that if he continues to misbehave, he will be replaced. Then do it.

The Unprepared ■ Repetition is the main point of rehearsal. The actor who doesn't remember blocking or who "forgets" to work on lines breaks everyone's concentration and disrupts the repetitive process. At the first readthrough, explain what preparation you expect. Then stick to it.

Some actors don't remember blocking because they don't write it down when it is given. Insist that all actors bring pencils (with erasers) to rehearsal and lay in a supply of loaners. Give enough time for people to jot down blocking.

However, most actors forget their blocking or fail to learn lines because they don't look at their scripts between rehearsals. Again, make your expectations clear from the outset: "You should know this blocking the next time we run this scene." Announce deadlines for the learning of lines—and stick to them. Ignore protests; most actors, when challenged to remember lines, do much better than they—or you—thought they could.

The Latecomer and No-Show ■ Habitual lateness or missed rehearsals could mean the actor has had a change in work hours or must get children fed and to the babysitter before leaving for rehearsal. Be sympathetic to legitimate problems, but keep in mind that the needs of the show come first. If accommodation cannot be made in the rehearsal schedule, replace the actor.

Before casting, have actors fill out a conflict sheet on which they can indicate any conflicts with rehearsal dates and times. After you cast the show, use these sheets to schedule rehearsals and as a kind of "contract" in case an actor comes to you later with a new conflict.

Some actors miss rehearsal because they think their role isn't that important and they won't be missed. This is often the case with ensemble members. They often respond best to a straightforward approach: "Martin, we missed you. We couldn't finish blocking the street scene because you weren't here. Be sure to be here tomorrow when we run through it again."

In many cases, you'll find peer pressure helpful. If rehearsal begins and Mary hasn't arrived, ask those who work with her to tell her how her absence has caused them inconvenience.

Make it clear you do not tolerate tardiness or absence. And remember, if the actors discover *you* aren't ready to rehearse at the appointed time, they soon will grow careless themselves.

The Show-Off ■ Some actors disrupt rehearsals by making jokes, mugging, or improvising inappropriate blocking or dialogue. This can be stopped quickly if you make a point of not laughing along, cutting in with a firm "Let's keep our attention on the play, Joel."

Show-Offs often have low self-esteem. The person wants—needs—to be noticed or thought clever. Find ways to praise such people when they do well. That way, you can channel their energy into constructive behavior.

The actor also may not know his lines or blocking, or feels uncomfortable in his role. See "The Unprepared" for the former; if you suspect the latter, talk to him in private. Offer to help him if he is insecure in his character.

Again, encouraging peer pressure may be a good tactic. When others in the company make it clear they don't appreciate his tactics, The Show-Off often reforms.

General Considerations

The word *director* implies giving orders. However, suggestions are psychologically neutral and thus helpful with many problem cases. A suggestion neither praises nor criticizes the actor; it merely opens the possibility of another way of playing a moment or scene. "Try going to the door on that line," you might suggest, or "How about playing against Sue's line here?," or "What would happen if Maggie laughed at Brick's story?"

Most actors have heightened egos and many are hypersensitive to boot. It's always a good rule to praise an actor in front of the cast and criticize him in private. The exception would be the overconfident actor who needs to be taken down a peg, or criticism that you can make general and apply to the whole cast.

20 | *Working with Inexperienced Actors*

It's Difficult, but Potentially Rewarding

*I*n her book, *Community Plays: How to Put Them On*, British playwright Ann Jellicoe describes in detail her experience directing most of the population of Dorchester, England, in a new play.

One of the problems peculiar to community theater, she writes, is dealing with inexperienced or outright bad actors who are "so unimaginative, so lacking in energy, that no matter what devices you use, you just don't seem to be helping them much."

"They will improve," she says. "It is your responsibility that the actor should never feel that he or she has failed."

That's a tall order, so we talked to a number of directors in community and educational theater to find out what ideas they had on this subject. Although there was no consensus on the best method to deal with "bad" actors, the suggestions that follow do offer some useful insights.

Poor acting results from many causes. It may be mental: a lack of confidence or inability to understand the needs of the scene, the character, or the plot. It may be physical: an inflexible body or voice, an inability to hear how one sounds or "see" what one looks like in action. In the worst case, it can be the result of all these problems.

The directors we talked with agreed that an actor doesn't have a chance to be good if he or she doesn't understand what is needed. One of the main tasks of rehearsal is to help people understand the meaning of what they are saying and what is needed to tell the story.

Several directors said they sometimes ask actors to put a speech into their own words to force them to think the meaning out. Others use improvisation and, when appropriate, a short talk on the historical or social conditions that surround the play, to help the actors understand why their characters are the way they are.

One director takes one rehearsal for a readthrough in which the actors pause after each line to explain the character's motivation. This can be a lengthy process, he admits, but it quickly tells him if the actors really understand their characters and how they relate to the action, and whether they comprehend the basic point of the play. The same process could be used with just one actor, he points out, with the director reading all the other lines.

When an actor's speaking voice lacks force and conviction, that's probably because that's the way they speak in real life. Their voices aren't strong or flexible because they seldom need to be much more expressive than "There's someone on the phone for you." In the theater, however, the actor may have to communicate all sorts of nuances with this same line. Going through the line-by-line interpretation discussed previously may help the actor find the proper inflection.

If an actor has a bad ear, one director has that actor speak lines into a tape recorder and play them back. "This works sort of like biofeedback," he says. "Have them read the line several different ways—tell them which words to emphasize, if necessary. Then play the tape back. Try to help them understand why one reading is better than the other. Then have them imitate their own inflection."

Another way is to select the key words that actually carry the meaning of their lines and emphasize them, giving the others less weight. This is a real help for those who deliver lines in a monotone. Verbs are especially important.

Finally, if you feel there is really no way the actor is ever going to succeed, alter the production. Give them lines or shouts against a storm or over loud music. If they can't speak loudly enough, don't deprive them of the line; get someone else on stage to repeat it. If all else fails, try distracting attention from the actor: have something else going on at the same time. Use the distraction positively, so the two simultaneous events compete or blend to raise the audience's interest.

Because it's extremely unlikely they will be in a large part, stick with them—don't abandon them. Support them with confidence and praise whenever you can, even if only for trying. The key to success in such situations resides in the working relationship established between director and actor. There is no way in the course of rehearsal that you can turn a novice actor into a seasoned performer, but you can help ensure the relationship is an effective one. Here's how.

Make a List ■ Start by assessing both the strong and weak points of the actor, then make a brief list of each in order of importance. This gives you a consistent working plan, something that will help you and the actor focus on the priorities. You may or may not get to work on every item on the list, but if you start with the most important, you're more sure of getting good results.

Emphasize Strengths ■ You cast the person for *some* reason. Perhaps it was that he or she looked the part, or sounded the part, or did something in auditions that you felt could be shaped into the character you wanted. In working with the actor, help emphasize what he or she does best, starting with the top items on your list. For example, if you cast an actor for the role of an energetic young man because he showed lots of energy at auditions, help him find ways to use that energy to build a believable character. If you cast a woman because she looked the part, help her focus on those physical characteristics that underscore her character.

Fix the Worst ■ Given your priority list, attack the number-one problem. Make this your consistent message. For example, one director told an actor, "You use your hands too much. It's distracting and out of character. From now on, you're restricted to two gestures—hands folded and hands down—unless otherwise directed." The director's notes at every rehearsal mentioned this point and the actor soon fixed it.

In another case, the actress was too young for the role and not able to project the character of a sophisticated woman of the world. The director decided to focus on the actress' walk and speech patterns. She worked separately with the actress, helping her to slow down her delivery and her walk. "Slow down everything you do," she said. "Your character wants everyone to notice her, so give them time to do so."

Sometimes the novice actor needs to be told *why* he is doing something. It's better to say "You're ashamed to look her in the eye, so you turn away," rather than simply, "Turn away from her."

If you try and try but the problem remains, you will have to resort to deemphasizing this weakness in some way. For example, if the actor is clumsy, you can change his or her blocking to disguise this fact. Then go on to the performer's second-most important weakness and try to deal with that.

Use Praise ■ Use praise lavishly, but not dishonestly. Bolster the actor when he or she does something well. But remember that others are observing—if you give praise when it's not deserved, they may lose trust in you when you praise *them*. Praise always can be given for trying: "Good! I could tell you were really concentrating that time. And you were speaking up much better, too. But I don't think we're quite there yet, do you? You see this bit here: What do you think she means when she's saying this?"

Emphasize Technique ■ Directing is teaching and one of your most valuable contributions is giving an actor some new understanding of technique that will improve the performance in this play and in those to come. One of the most common problems in novices is the inability to portray a particular emotion. In this case, try giving the actor some physical business, movement, body positions, or gestures that are characteristic of the emotion you want. In this way, the *doing* may evoke the *feeling*. You also can show the actor the mood, intensity, and feeling you want without actually reading the lines. You might improvise around the lines so the actor can see the possibilities of the scene without imitating directly what you have done.

Show Them How ■ When all else fails, or time is short, you have to *tell* the actor what to do, or better, show him. This presupposes you can demonstrate effectively (some directors can't) and that the actor is capable of mimicking you. Because this type of direction takes more time, it may be wise to schedule a special rehearsal for just you and the actor. If the role is a large one, you may want to focus on those scenes most vital to the play. Sometimes you can show the actor the way he has just done something and then show him the way *you* think it should be done. Then ask, "Which do you think was more effective?"

21 | The Tortoise and the Hare

With Experienced Actors, Different Strokes for Different Folks

Actor-writer Simon Callow divides all actors into hares and tortoises, sculptors or bricklayers. Anyone who has directed more than a few shows should recognize the types to which Callow refers.

"The hares," he writes, "tear off, paraphrasing, acting in broad strokes, alarming you by their infidelity to the text and the grossness of their gestures." The tortoises, on the other hand, "proceed timidly but accurately, not moving on till they've solved each problem, alarming you by their laboriousness and their inability to take the plunge.

"Sculptors," he continues, "drag messy sprawling piles of raw material into the rehearsal room, flinging themselves at it with their bare hands or a hammer and chisel, giving no impression whatever of a possible end result, while bricklayers come in . . . with a wheelbarrow full of regular wellmade bricks that they methodically lay one on top of another."

It is the director's task to make the most out of the actors' capabilities. However, because each actor brings a different style and experience to the production, that can be difficult work at best. That's why it's so important to recognize the different creative styles of the actors you are working with—and how to put those different styles to work.

While Callow's taxonomy is vividly accurate, one could just as easily say that actors are divided into those who work from the outside in and those who work from the inside out.

"I recently worked with a man and a woman [we'll call them Scott and Lisa] who were supposed to fall in love during the course of the play," a director tells us. "They were to begin by not liking each other and work toward a moment of revelation when they realize they are meant for one another.

"But Scott was the type of actor who builds his character from the inside. Every movement, every bit of business, every line delivery had to square with his idea of the character. It was impossible to block scenes quickly, because he questioned so much. Actually, I appreciated his dedication, and many of his suggestions were excellent, but the delay he caused was aggravating, and Lisa was about to clobber him. Lisa's the type who creates a role from the outside in. Give her blocking and a rough idea of how she should deliver her lines and she'll learn them. *Then* she'll work out the motivation. Later, if something doesn't feel right, she'll ask me for clarification or maybe a change. With Scott, I could see him building his characterization from the start; with Lisa, it all came together the last week of rehearsal.

"It was like a husband and wife with two completely different biorhythms, two completely different views of the world. My job was to keep things moving so that both of them would feel comfortable with their parts and with each other. It wasn't easy."

The turning point came when the director asked Scott to stay after rehearsal.

"I told him how good he was, how good the show was going to be. I also told him about Lisa and *her* creative needs. I knew he was a perfectionist, so I said to him, 'You're going to be able to play this so much better if Lisa feels comfortable. Right now, she needs to understand the continuity of the play. I appreciate your wanting to make things better. So to keep things moving, how about us talking after the rehearsals? If you have a concern or an idea to bring up, we'll talk about it, and if it seems workable, we'll go with it.' He agreed, and it really worked.

"By the end of a rehearsal, he couldn't remember every little thing that had bothered him, and the things he did remember usually were important enough to deserve discussion. Sometimes I overruled him, but oftentimes I went with his ideas. Meanwhile, Lisa had the continuity she needed, and the rehearsals became far less wearing. True, I sometimes had to stay afterwards and deal with Scott, but it was worth it. By opening night, I was really tired, but the actors weren't, and frankly they're the ones the audience pays to see."

The moral in this extended story (with names changed to protect the egos involved) is simple. Rehearsal is a patch of ground on which the flower of art ultimately will grow. Be at the ready with the right fertilizer and a good hoe—or you may end up with weeds.

Helping Them Be Heard | 22

Projection Is a Special Challenge for Many Actors

DIANE CREWS

*M*ost of us who work in children's theater would probably agree that, in general, projection is a problem. Indeed, it's a problem that affects many high school and community groups as well. There are many reasons for this:

■ Poor to nonexistent acoustic design in performance spaces. I tour shows into schools, churches, and community centers. Maybe one in fifteen of these facilities has adequate acoustics.

■ Sound technology (microphones and amplifiers) has made projection unnecessary. Actors believe, therefore, that they don't have to project.

■ Schools of acting, which for many years focused on the emotional/psychological/interior realities of the character, omitted teaching the basic acting skills of being seen and heard. This is turning around again, but many directors working now were part of those schools.

■ There's a lack of importance placed on good, clear speech in this country, and this is emphasized by the role models offered via the media.

How do you help actors, of any age, to project? If you had six months to a year, and didn't have a show to do, you could teach them relaxation, strengthening, breathing, and projection techniques.

Few of us working with inexperienced actors have that luxury. We have five to six amazingly short weeks of rehearsal. During this time, lines, blocking, music, dancing, and a myriad number of things the script might require must be taught. Many members of your cast not only will be young, but also will be first-timers. So you must start with basic stage geography, playing open, and staying in character lessons.

If this sounds like a directorial excuse, it is not. I'm merely pointing out that we can't possibly give our inexperienced actors the kind of training that some of us gained during four to eight years of higher education and performing in hundreds of roles.

So what's a director to do? Give up? *No!* Here are a few suggestions. These are tips other directors and I have learned from necessity.

■ From the audition on, continually request that actors speak louder, slow down, and enunciate. Problems with projection, speed, and pronunciation contribute to our inability to hear and understand.

■ Do not allow actors to be fooled by the size of the rehearsal space. No matter how intimate that space is, never let up on the need to project. If you stop demanding projection, they'll stop projecting. You must keep up the request until projection has become automatic for the actor. You'll be able to hear when that occurs.

■ Let the actors experience a similar size space to that in which they ultimately will perform. If nothing is available, take them outside. I always take the entire cast, as early in the rehearsal period as possible, to the theater. The cast will assemble in a line across the front of the stage. From the back of the house I "interview" each character. If you've asked the actor three times to speak louder (you've probably goofed in casting), don't give up. Simply try speaking at *their* level when you ask the next question. This usually makes your point quite nicely.

■ You cannot wait until they get on stage to give them this experience. Our theater has only one week or so turnaround time between mainstage and children's productions. We often open with only three rehearsals, including techs, in the space. It's almost impossible to do projection work while dealing with lights, costumes, set changes, and more.

■ Finally, when all else fails, I also use a hanging mike and two floor mikes, plus a few body mikes for soloists in musicals. Sound equipment usually can be borrowed from your local high school or rented fairly reasonably. Am I copping out? No, I'm being realistic. The audience must hear the playwright's words. The majority of inexperienced actors have not yet developed their projection ability, and most theaters are acoustically lacking. Let's face it, all the stars are miked. There are no Ethel Mermans left, I fear.

23 | *Triumphing over Mumblers*

Practical Tips to Help Your Actors Project to the Last Row in the Theater

SARAH ANNE STARR

G ood projection is fundamental, and it's the director's responsibility to help actors project. But what
specific preparations can directors have actors do
to help them triumph over mumbling? What exercises can they use so the actors can communicate with the
audience members in the very last row?

Here are several exercises I've developed over the years
to help actors triumph over mumbling.

Breathing

Having spent their lives breathing successfully from their
upper chests, actors sometimes rebel against putting out
more effort. Explain to them the clear correlation between
correct breathing and projection. The benefits of correct—
and therefore easier—breathing include increased breath
capacity, enhanced self-confidence, and a throat freed from
tension. (A performer's throat should not hurt, even after a
long scene.)

Ask your actors: When they breathe normally, are their

chest and shoulders rising? Does their stomach contract when they breathe in?

Correct breathing is like a sponge taking on water: It expands when taking in the liquid; it contracts when letting go of the water. Unlike shallow-chest breathing, diaphragmatic breathing when inhaling is exaggerated. Not just your rib cage, but also your stomach expands. (You may wish not to differentiate between diaphragmatic and "belly" breathing.) Pull your shirt tight against your sides so the actors can see you expand sideways as well as in front when you breathe correctly.

Start your rehearsal with simple stretches. As you stretch, have the actors yawn, relaxing their throats. Progress to inhaling with a yawn and exhaling on an "Ahhhhhhh." This "Ah" will usually be produced correctly; your goal is to encourage all sounds to be made this way.

Next, everyone marches in a circle. As you walk, inhale for four steps, exhale for four steps, and repeat. Each time, attempt to completely fill and completely empty your lungs. Increase the number of steps as the actors develop proper breathing habits.

Have each cast member hold a finger a few inches from their mouth, and attempt to blow it out as if it were a candle. They should keep a steady stream focused on their finger as long as possible. Alternatively, change the exhaled breath to a hiss.

Have them repeat the word *Ha!* as loudly as they can without shouting. Their stomach should bounce. The actors should try this both as a single *ha* and as ten *ha*'s per breath.

On a single note, have them hold a hum, then open it to an *ah*: "Hmmmmahhmmmmahhhhmmmmahh." Repeat with other vowel sounds: ay, ee, oh, oo.

Now change to an open-mouthed hum: "Hhnnnnggggggg-ah." Again, repeat with other vowels. Tell them to feel the vibration—the resonance—in the nose.

As your actors accept these exercises, zero in on problems during rehearsals. If an actor is not projecting, stop the rehearsal and have him say a few "ha"s or "hnngg-ay"s. Occasionally recruit an audience from those not currently on stage, asking them to raise their hands whenever an actor is too quiet and cannot be heard quickly.

Enunciation

Most mumblers not only speak quietly, but also have trouble with the correct placement and shape of consonants and vowels. Discuss the three kinds of consonants (explosive, aspirate, and vowel-formation) with your cast and draw attention to the difference between voiced and unvoiced.

Have them place their hands on their Adam's apple. With voiced consonants, correctly formed, they will feel a vibration. The explosive consonants, like B, P, D, T, G, K, J, and CH, can be both voiced and unvoiced. (B is a voiced consonant in the word *butter* and P is its unvoiced equivalent in the word *putter*; likewise, the pairs D and T, G and K, and J and CH.) Aspirates, like H (*height*) and WH (*why*), are unvoiced, as are vowel-formation consonants like W (*wish*) and Y (*yes*).

Actors' difficulties in enunciation often include beginning consonants, final consonants, and tongue-twisters. Practice these with specific exercises, first in groups, then individually, one after another. You can use traditional tongue-twisters such as, "Around the rugged rocks, the ragged rascal ran"; "How happily Howard hops!"; or "Jason cheers, but Charles jeers", or make up your own.

During exercises, focus on hitting every consonant, beginning and ending. When the exercise deals with a related pair, such as P and B, emphasize the difference.

Performance

Often, mumblers are simply not at ease in front of an audience of strangers. Perhaps they fear being laughed at or worry they appear ridiculous. Both in speech and in action, they then avoid animation to the point of monotony.

When dealing with timid actors, refrain from throwing them into situations where they must create. Improvisation exercises may paralyze them. Rather than throwing them on an empty stage with no directions, provide the dialogue and ask them to communicate through it. Beginning Dr. Seuss books, with their large print and simple but colorful words, are ideal. Adults, especially, will feel silly reading "Mr. Brown can moo. Can you?" in a serious monotone, and will begin to perform.

Discuss the difference between a dull, tense actor and one who is hamming it up. Point out that an actor who appears nervous is inviting far more criticism than the actor who simulates confidence and animation. Then challenge your actors to magnify every emotion, tempo, and dynamic change. While this won't necessarily cure all mumbling, in many cases the extra zing does translate to clearer, louder speech. Even in a serious play, you may find that what the actor considers overdone is exactly what you want. Be sure to explain in what ways the expressive performance is superior to their normal lack of clarity.

Once your actors are comfortable with their lines—and one another—you can interrupt rehearsals whenever mumbling begins. This is important: If you allow such problems to continue, they will become an ingrained part of an actor's character.

Clear lines, projected well, are a necessity. Insist upon them, and watch your play—and your audience—benefit.

24 | Past Tense

Advice and Exercises to Help Actors Rid Themselves of Nervousness

SARAH ANNE STARR

*T*he first five or ten minutes of a play are crucial. Actors' energy must be focused, their bodies and voices tuned to the needs of the performance.

Nervousness and tension can cause crippling inhibitions, especially during a play's opening scene. Nervous actors unconsciously restrict their movements, vocal range, and projection. For those all-important moments, they're wooden. The result can be painful—not only for the actor, but also for the audience.

No matter what the specific manifestation of the nervousness, the solution is relaxation. If your actors aren't relaxed, not only will they look unnatural, but they also will breathe improperly, which creates more stress and tension. Proper breathing, on the other hand, induces relaxation, which causes correct breathing. Teach your cast the difference between useful energy and destructive tension.

What's the difference? Destructive tension is unfocused energy; it comes between the actor and the role being played. *Focused* energy, on the other hand, is useful energy.

"If we remember that the tensions and excitement that grip the actor are in part the body's means of preparing for a challenging situation," points out Stanley Kahan in his text, *Introduction to Acting*, "then it is clear that the person under tension is actually better equipped to handle the exacting demands of acting."

Acting demands a tremendous output of energy—controlled energy. That kind of energy can come only from a body ready for the challenge of the performance. And as contrary as it may sound, that body must be relaxed. Just as runners must stretch and relax muscles to prepare for a race, actors must stretch and relax to prepare for their hour (more or less) on the stage.

Here are nine relaxation exercises for the body and mind your actors can use. Schedule the exercises as close to performance time as you can to avoid stress rebuilding after them. Notice that this list begins with exercises that exaggerate tension—the reason is that nervous actors relax from a state of extreme rigidity more easily than they can from their "normal" tension.

1. *Full-body explosion*: Sit arm's distance from your neighbor. Taking a deep breath, contract every muscle in your body. Clench your fists. Draw your arms and legs up tight against your chest. Tighten your muscles during the entire three- to five-second inhaling period. Then, all at once, let it out, exhaling with a loud sigh. As you exhale, "explode" from the fetal position, releasing your facial muscles as well as your arms and legs.

2. *Shoulder shrugs*: On an inhale, bring your shoulders high and squeeze them tightly for three to five seconds. Then, on a fast exhale, drop your shoulders. Repeat. You also can alternate: first shrug the left shoulder, then the right.

3. *Arm shakes*: While standing, drop your hands to your sides. Swing your arms from front to back ten to fifteen times. Make fists, then relax them. Take a deep breath. On the exhale, shake your hands and fingers vigorously from the shoulders and elbows.

4. *Leg shakes*: Stand near a wall for support. Lift one leg slightly from the floor. Curl your toes into a "fist," then relax them. Repeat. Shake your leg from the ankle, then knee, then hip. Breathe throughout. Switch legs.

5. *Head rolls*: Studies show that rolling your head in complete circles may be harmful. Instead, inhale while closing your eyes, then lower your head left on the exhale. Relax your neck. Repeat three times. During each deep breath, take your head to a different side (right, front, or back). Keep your movements slow and relaxed.

6. *Stretch*: Standing with your feet together, stretch from the waist to your right. Don't bounce. Keep it slow and remember to breathe. Return to an upright position and repeat to the left. Straighten again. Inhale, relaxing. Exhale, reaching for the ceiling. Stretch! Inhale, returning your arms to your sides. Relax.

7. *Rag doll*: Reach for the floor, bending from the waist. Relax your neck, head, and arms, letting them all drop forward. Take deep breaths, slowing down and relaxing a little more with each exhale. Try to loosen every joint in your body. Continue until you are completely limp and hanging down. Then slowly, vertebra by vertebra, straighten back up.

Now that your actors' bodies are relaxed, switch to mental and emotional relaxation. Have them sit or lie down in a comfortable position. Focus on breathing. Slow it down and breathe from the abdomen rather than the chest. With eyes closed, inhale through your nose. Inhale as long as you can, then hold it up to five seconds. Through your mouth, exhale completely (slowly). Repeat several times. Then try one or both of the following visualization exercises.

8. *Visual vacation*: As you inhale, picture a gentle summer afternoon on the beach. (Directors: Describe whatever scene you feel would be appropriate; this is just one example.) The sun is warm on your face and hair, on your arms, your legs. Your body is heavy, as though you're almost asleep. The sand beneath you is soft. The waves are rhythmically lapping at the beach. The sound of birds is in the distance. Inhale. Exhale. With each easy breath, inhale the air of this soothing place. Feel the relaxation in every part of your body. From your feet to your face, feel yourself growing calmer. Now take one last breath. Hold it. Let it out slowly, and open your eyes.

9. *Pulling the plug on tension*: Picture your body as a sink full of water, with the drain holes in your hands and feet. As you breathe, imagine the water going down the drain. Picture your body emptying of water, starting with your head and neck, and going down until there are just shallow pools remaining at your feet. The water swirls silently out, leaving your body empty and clean. Now—inhale energy into your empty body. Fill up with fresh, invigorating energy that will help you concentrate, project, and do your best possible job.

Leading your actors through these exercises before each performance will reduce tension and help focus the actors' energy where it belongs—on acting.

And a Final Tip

Keep it up! Relaxation is cumulative. Encourage your actors to relax consciously while waiting backstage. Ten deep, slow breaths just before an entrance will help them return to the relaxed state their exercises produced.

Having Words with Your Actors

25

Twelve Ways to Criticize Effectively

*F*or better or worse, directing is by nature a critical process, weeding out the bad and reinforcing the good. Sometimes you can achieve your purpose with an actor through the use of positive comment. However, it is impossible—and foolish—to avoid criticism when it is the most appropriate action. Here are twelve guidelines to remember the next time you have to tell someone he or she has done something wrong.

1. *Identify the behavior you want to criticize.* Direct your criticism at the action, not the person.

2. *Make criticism specific.* Not "You're always late to rehearsal," but rather "You were late Tuesday and Wednesday and put us behind."

3. *Be sure the behavior you're criticizing can be changed.* One director screamed (already one strike against him) at a cast member for not knowing her lines. Later, he found out she had a learning disability.

4. *Use "I" and "we" to emphasize that you want to work out the problem together,* rather than making threats.

5. *Make sure the other person understands the reason for your criticism.* Otherwise, the actor may think you have something personal against him or are just being difficult yourself.

6. *Don't belabor the point.* Keep criticism short and sweet; no lectures.

7. Unless there is some good reason, *don't criticize in public.* Humiliating people usually is not a good way to help them accept the need for change.

8. *Don't set a tone of anger or sarcasm.* Both are counterproductive.

9. *Show the person you understand his or her feelings.*

10. *Start off by saying something good.* Do not use the word *but* to introduce the negative—it sets up the person to reject both the positive comment you have just given and the negative one you're about to deliver. In other words, instead of saying, "You're very good in this scene, but I think you need to go over your lines more carefully," try "You're very good in this scene, and you'll make it work if you go over your lines more carefully."

11. *Offer incentives for changed behavior.* Offer to help the person correct the problem if you can.

12. At the end, *reaffirm your support and confidence in the actor.*

Avoiding Personality Conflicts

How to Keep the Communication Lines Open

26

A ny communication failure between actor and director is a two-way street. Often the problem is what is commonly called a personality conflict, but this term suggests there is nothing either of you can do about the situation. Actually, you may be able to do quite a lot, given the right tools. Psychological studies show that people approach or react to problems in markedly different ways. One simple and useful model divides people into three types: Thinkers, Doers, and Feelers.

The Thinker won't take action immediately, preferring to sort out the possibilities beforehand. In contrast, The Doer's first response to a problem is to take action, even if that action doesn't solve the problem. After all, one always can try something else.

Feelers try to solve a problem by "what feels right," either to themselves or to the others involved with the situation.

You can imagine the conflict that arises when a Thinker-actor is teamed up with a Doer-director, for example. The actor may spend a great deal of time working on his characterization or questioning his motivation. The director is just trying to get the show on the boards. The director thinks the actor is impeding progress. The actor thinks the director is insensitive or putting too much pressure on him.

On the other hand, a Feeler-director may be so worried about hurting people's feelings that he doesn't take charge. A Thinker-director may spend so much time analyzing the play that she never completes a working plan. A Doer-actor may improvise constantly, looking for a solution to his character's motivation.

One good way to resolve or avoid a personality conflict is to determine your personality types. That way, you'll know the sort of behavior patterns that will conflict with your own. You can watch for them and be prepared to react constructively.

For example, Feelers often assume emotional content in another person's actions and may feel threatened by what they consider aggressive behavior. But if the other person is a Doer, his actions may simply be his on-the-spot solution to a problem. Doers very often have little or no emotional investment in their actions; theirs is simply a pragmatic approach. So, once they have done their thing, suggest another solution. If it works, they are likely to go along with you.

Avoiding conflict means being prepared. If you are a Doer-director working with a Thinker-actor, make sure your suggestions show your "doing" has some thought behind it. Don't say, "Do it this way"; instead suggest, "I think Joe would be afraid to walk to the door that quickly." So, the next time you start work on a production, give some thought to your own personality and to each of the people with whom you'll be working. You may find life a lot easier.

GENERAL CONCERNS

*M*any issues that a director may face are not wrapped up in the specifics of design or in the interpretation of lines. Rather, they can be found in the day-to-day in dealing with the myriad complexities and personalities associated with a production. This section takes a look at the most important of these.

27 | A Chemistry Lesson

Sometimes Being a Good Director Means Being a Good Manager

A front-page article in the *Wall Street Journal* said that of most American managers who lose their jobs, half are fired for "bad personal chemistry."

Personal chemistry is important in any managerial situation, including directing a show. Like most directors, you can profit by improving your supervisory skills. This is true even if you have an advanced degree, years of experience, and general good character. Some directors don't realize that good supervisory skills contribute to the success of a production. Others have never learned. And sometimes under the pressure of the moment, we slip into some self-defeating behaviors. Here, then, are fourteen basic supervisory dos and don'ts you need to know—and use—to be a successful director.

1. *Get to know your cast and crew.* They're human beings with differing personalities, feelings, ambitions, and circumstances. You'll win their commitment only if you understand them and treat them as individuals.

2. *Don't expect your people to read your mind.* Even the truly obvious may need to be mentioned at least once, if only to make sure everyone is on the same wavelength.

3. *Explain why.* Creative people by nature are uncomfortable with doing something a certain way just because you tell them so. By explaining, you help them understand your underlying concept and often elicit good ideas to strengthen it.

4. *Don't blame others for your mistakes.* When people who have followed your instructions produce results that aren't right, don't castigate them. They only did what you told them to do. They know that, and they'll resent your attempt to shift the blame. Remember, we tend to sympathize with and respect those who are honest about their own failings.

5. *Praise where it's merited.* While most people think they are generous with praise, studies indicate most people don't think their supervisors give enough. This holds true in the theater as well. If someone is doing well, make sure you make a note of it and let the person know.

6. *Give feedback.* Don't delay this step so long that you reach the point where something needs a major overhaul or redirection. Feedback allows people to pick up nuances that continually help them improve their performance. Even when the talent is troubled, many could—and would—do much better if you gave them regular guidance.

7. *Share information.* Don't neglect to pass on information that affects your cast and crew. Your whole relationship with them is based on trust. When they learn through the grapevine something you should have told them, they realize you didn't care much about them. At that point, you've damaged their loyalty and their trust in you.

8. *Listen.* You don't know everything. Give people opportunities to respond to your plans or come up with ideas. You may learn about something important that's going on, a suggestion to improve the production, or about developing problems. Make time and keep yourself available for such opportunities.

9. *Don't play favorites.* Treating everyone equally in major situations is not enough. If you're unfair in minor everyday situations, people are sure to notice it. That means you should not excuse one person's absence, lateness, or failure to deliver while making clear how unhappy you are when someone else commits the same offense.

10. *Control the constant urge to demonstrate you are the boss.* Everyone already knows that. You don't have to one-up, add to, or somehow change all your cast and crew's suggestions, or work to

prove it. By showing a consistent passion for having the last word on everything, you easily can frustrate and eventually discourage creativity in others.

11. *Learn to delegate.* If you try to do everything, you cease to be a good director. You need time to focus on the important factors of pacing and characterization. If you're also trying to handle other administrative tasks, you are robbing your cast and crew of your overall stewardship. To delegate successfully, you must be willing to give people the authority they need to carry out assignments. As long as they fulfill their responsibilities and are in sync with your overall vision, let them work in their own way.

12. *Avoid verbal shocks.* Despite the big changes in standards during the last several decades, many people still take offense at profanity, dirty jokes, and blasphemy. In addition, this kind of behavior will tend to make you look juvenile, as if you haven't yet figured out adult ways to express yourself—and who could feel comfortable with such a director?

13. *Don't confuse cordiality and intimacy.* Frankly, it's hard to be a director and a friend. It's best to state at the outset that while you want a friendly atmosphere, you also want it clear that as director your word is final—which leads us to the last point:

14. *Don't concentrate on being popular.* Of course, you don't want to alienate anyone, and of course you want to be liked—but in the right way and for the right reasons. Good direction is not a popularity contest. Your actors don't really want you to be a buddy; they look to you for guidance and a controlling vision. If you concentrate on being fair, offering guidance and rewards, you'll be respected and liked. And that's the only kind of popularity that will guarantee your directing is both productive and pleasant.

Lighten Up
Seven Ideas for
Boosting Morale

28

*H*ere are some ideas for rewarding cast and crew members, as well as other volunteers. All are from actual experiences of production personnel.

1. *Be appreciative.* "More people said 'Thank you' to me tonight than say it in six weeks at my job," said one volunteer after she beamed a flashlight on the dark steps so no one would trip backstage. "It seems obvious we should be polite to each other," remarked a production staff member about this incident, "but often in those last nights before opening, we forget. Note the small efforts and reward them with thanks and a smile."

2. *Make sure cast and crew know each other.* The simplest way is for the director to take time to introduce the technical crew to the cast on the first appropriate night in the theater.

3. *Get ceremonial.* Opening and closing nights have their own momentum and usually don't need morale boosting. Sprinkle small ceremonies throughout a production. One performer, known for his inability to dance, was presented with a pair of thrift-shop shoes the night after he had mastered a particularly difficult routine. Both shoes were for the left foot.

4. *Have an initiation.* One man recalls being playfully held down while the stage manager painted a green stripe on his jeans. The identifying stripe showed he belonged. "I felt respected, relied on, and welcome," he says.

5. *It's the thought that counts.* Expensive gifts are usually inappropriate and can lead to jealousy. Small gestures often carry more weight. One director was delighted with a two-ounce bottle of gin and a tin of aspirin as a "survival kit." Anything bearing your company logo is welcome—a tee-shirt, a scarf, a sweatshirt, or whatever. A plain white towel with the company logo on it was presented to a company member who quickly dubbed it her "crying towel," to be passed out as needed to other company members.

6. *Start a contest.* Have the cast submit nominations for the best quote during rehearsal. One company, producing *H.M.S. Pinafore,* even put the quote (from the director, in this case) in the program: "Hey, guys, this isn't Chekhov, you know!" In another case, a particularly bad publicity photo (one that wasn't used) was posted with a prize given for the best caption.

7. *Above all, build morale by keeping a sense of humor.* One musical director, exasperated two nights before opening, resorted to unseemly shouting. At the end of his tirade he added sheepishly, "You'll all be glad to know I feel much better now." This owning up to his bad behavior brought laughter and applause, restoring goodwill and allowing performers to go back to work with renewed energy.

Onstage and Backstage Behavior

29

Etiquette, Schmetiquette—
It All Boils Down
to One Thing

*E*tiquette, the dictionary says, refers to "the forms and manners established by convention as acceptable or required in social relations or profession." Luckily, the rules of theatrical etiquette spring from one simple concern—to avoid anything that might impair or weaken the performance.

Many directors take it for granted that cast and crew understand the rules of the theater. Yet this isn't always the case—and not all problems arise in amateur theater. Liv Ullmann writes in her autobiography that while appearing in *I Remember Mama* in New York, she was startled to see a gorilla in the wings. Alarmed, she managed to get through her scenes. As she left the stage, she discovered it was a crew member in disguise.

In community and educational theater, it is a good idea to explain the rules of onstage and backstage behavior at least once. Then it's the director or stage manager's role to make sure these rules are followed—not only by actors, but also by every member of the production staff.

Here are our Ten Commandments of Theater Etiquette:

1. *Thou shalt not distract onstage performers.* This means no making of faces, gestures, or anything else that can affect their performance.

2. *Thou shalt not intentionally alter blocking or lines.* Acting is teamwork in its greatest sense. To do anything that might upset the concentration of another performer is atrocious conduct.

3. *Thou shalt not be seen or heard by the audience except when directed.* When offstage, be certain to stay out of sight. Watch carefully for set pieces and props. Better yet, stay out of the wings entirely unless you are about to go on.

4. *Thou shalt not play practical jokes before or during performance.* Onstage pranks are bad enough, but anything that distracts an actor from his or her performance is a Bad Thing.

5. *Thou shalt not invite visitors backstage before the show or during intermission.* Such visitors get in the way, distract from concentration, and are, in general, plain nuisances. Someone should be present to escort these people off the premises.

6. *Thou shalt not appear in the lobby or other public place in makeup or costume before the show or during intermission.* The illusion of reality is a fragile thing, and it is harmful for the production to call attention to the unreality outside the theater. (After the play is a different matter.)

7. *Thou shalt not eat or drink in costume.* It doesn't take much cola or coffee to put a noticeable stain on a gown or pair of pants. While being careful is a start, abstinence is the best prevention. And while we're on the matter, no food or drink in the wings, either. This goes for stage crew as well.

8. *Thou shalt not watch from the wings unless thou art about to go on.* Otherwise, you are in the way of the backstage crew and other actors.

9. *Thou shalt not do anything that does not bear direct, necessary relation to what is going on on stage during a performance.* The best performance is a focused one, and most actors find it impossible to return fully to character when distracted by nontheatrical backstage activities.

10. *Commit thyself equally to each performance.* You may perform a play many times, but each member of the audience probably will see it only once. Make sure they are getting the best-quality performance possible.

It's a good idea to post the rules where all can see, and to ask everyone to read them. That way, no one will have an excuse for behaving in any way that may put a show in jeopardy.

Backstage

Now let's take a look at the etiquette of the dressing room, green room, and other backstage areas.

1. *No Visitors, Please* ■ Concentration, writes Doug Moston in his book, *Coming to Terms with Acting*, is "the ability or act of focusing all your attention or energy where you want or need it." Thus, anything that interferes with actors' concentration can damage their performance—and the show.

That is why people not involved in the production must not be allowed backstage until after the performance. Visitors are at best a needless distraction, and at worst a downright nuisance.

A note in the program and a large sign at the backstage door takes care of the majority of would-be visitors. There are others, however, who may demand special attention. For example, a "No Visitors" sign is sometimes ignored by company members who aren't in the current production, but who feel free to come backstage because they feel they are "a member of the family." The truth is, each production develops its own sense of family, a dynamic that can be compromised by even a friendly outsider. Any backstage visitor must be either greeted or ignored—and either way, that takes some energy on the part of the performers who are preparing for the show.

Akin to the "We're not visitors—we're family" ploy is the cast or crew member who brings along a child. Of course, emergency situations do arise (the sitter doesn't show up), but in general, children who are not part of the production do not belong in the green room or dressing room. They quickly grow bored, get underfoot, and in the way. They may pose a danger to themselves or others. And when their parent is on stage or helping with the set, they either go unsupervised or divert the energy of cast members. Forget the "You won't even know they're here" ploy. You most assuredly will.

2. *Keep It Down* ■ Einstein once said energy can be neither created nor destroyed. That is not true backstage, however. Here energy *is* created—both the positive, focused kind that helps drive the performance and the negative kind produced by such simple but often overlooked stressors as noise.

Therefore, radios or stereos don't belong. Let's face it—it's almost impossible to find music *everybody* likes, so it's bound to bother someone. In addition, simple conversation has to compete with the sound level, with actors speaking louder or straining to be heard. More important, ambient noise can obscure important communication—such as the stage manager's warning of "Places, please!"

By the same token, it's wise to ask actors to keep their voices down and save their energy for the stage. Those who do vocal warmups should go into the restroom or outside. However, there is one important exception—if the cast does vocal warmups as a group, the focus on the performance is maintained and strengthened.

3. *Stay Focused* ■ During the show, card games and the like can help pass the time, but unless you're doing one of those big shows where the ensemble has twenty minutes or more between entrances, actors are usually better off conserving their energy and focusing on their next entrance. Card games also may lead to loud conversations that can fray the voice and, in some cases, be heard from the house.

There is a great deal less of this kind of thing with one theater company we know. The reason: A video monitor has been installed and the cast can watch the show from the green room. This not only reduces the number of people watching from the wings, but also keeps the actors more focused on the progress of the show.

4. *Respect Their Space* ■ It's simple courtesy not to shove others' clothes or personal items out of the way to make room for your own. If there is a shortage of space, the stage manager should call everyone together to brainstorm a mutually acceptable solution.

Respecting others' space also means actors need to clean up after themselves. Dealing with another person's mess is an unnecessary stressor that can affect the quality of your performance—and affect everyone in the show.

Respect others' mental space as well. For example, some actors prefer to be quiet before a performance. Be sensitive to this and don't try to strike up a conversation.

The great Italian actress Anna Magnani, whose emotional vitality was never in need of stimulation, used to work alone on a crossword puzzle before every performance because, she said, it was her *mind* that needed waking up.

5. *When It's Better to Wait* ■ An actress in heavy conversation in the dressing room did not hear her cue and was seriously late for an

entrance. By not paying attention, she caused the show to stumble and created momentary panic among the other performers. That was problem enough, but it was compounded when she was bawled out as soon as she left the stage. Her subsequent performance was over-heated and out of control as she worked off her anger.

While it may seem logical to deal with bad behavior immediately, it's better for the show if you wait until after the final curtain. You'll be in control of your temper and will have had time to phrase your comments to best advantage. (In this case, a chewing-out was prob-ably unnecessary. The actress in question was well aware of her transgression and its effect on her fellow actors.)

6. *Don't Move* ■ "I came backstage to make a quick change," re-calls one actor, "and my costume wasn't where I'd left it before the show started. I broke into a sweat, I panicked. I hunted for several minutes, and with my dresser's help finally found it—on another rack where someone had moved it without telling me. I barely made my change in time, and when I walked out onto the stage I was still jit-tery and—well, I stunk."

Thus, this simple rule: Don't move anything belonging to some-one else without permission. Actors must be confident that when they look for a costume or reach for a prop they have placed off stage, it will be there. The moment of panic may be only brief, but who needs it?

"I once shared a hat with another actor," another actor told us. "I wore the hat in Act One, he wore it in Act Two. My head being larger than his, at final dress rehearsal he stuck paper toweling in the lining around the brim so it would fit better. However, he didn't tell me what he'd done and I didn't notice the padding when I put it on as I walked on stage opening night. I was baffled as the hat mysteriously refused to stay on my head. It rattled me and I —well, I stunk."

7. *Loose Lips Sink Shows* ■ "Guess who's going to be in the house tonight?" an actor yelled as he came in the green room door. The celebrity was a well-known director, and you can imagine how the news of his presence affected some of the performers. One forgot her lines; another actually padded his part.

Ask the cast not to discuss who's in the audience and certainly not to scan the audience for familiar faces to share with the others. The actor's focus should be on what's happening on stage, not out in the house.

Backstage also is not a group-therapy session. Actors need to remember their personal lives are just that—personal. There are always exceptions, of course. Sometimes a traumatic event must be acknowledged. For the most part, however, it's best to leave one's troubles outside. Psychiatrists often encourage patients to become other-directed, to move beyond the preoccupation with self. How better to do that than in the ensemble environment of the theater?

8. *The Golden Rule* ■ Probably the best advice regarding back-stage etiquette is simply to practice the Golden Rule: Treat others as you want to be treated and keep in mind why you're there.

The actor's relation to the play, writes Simon Callow, "is that of rider to horse. *It* is the energy," he says, "you are the direction. You must be above it and on top of it."

Allowing the actor to focus on the performance is at the heart of these backstage rules of behavior. After all, the actors *are* the performance.

Dealing with Bad Reviews | 30

Helping Actors Deal with—and Learn from—Criticism

One situation every director faces at least once is helping the cast deal with a negative review. While you must judge the situation based on your knowledge of the individuals involved, here are some suggestions summarized from the responses of a number of directors we queried.

■ *Don't overreact.* It's easy to become angry or anxious after reading a negative review, but things are seldom as bad as you imagine once you get to the theater. Actors have a way of boosting their own morale backstage. In terms of preventive medicine, you can see why it's important to build a family feeling among your cast and crew: A close-knit company invariably will close ranks and protect its own.

■ *Get it out in the open.* Don't pretend nothing's happened. Call the cast together and help them understand that a review is only one person's opinion, and not yours or that of the audience. If appropriate, help them learn from the review how to improve their performance. Or, as one director said, "Tell your cast to go out and prove to the audience the critic was absolutely wrong." If the review singles out a particular actor, talk to that person immediately. If you disagree with the review, tell your actors so, and why—particularly if you don't want them to change their performance.

■ *Don't go it alone.* Over ten years, one company suffered negative reviews from one newspaper critic. Invariably, the review would target one actor as the focus of the critical barbs. Since the critic's last name was Simon, the company created an "award" built around a can of car wax, in honor of the actor who had been "Simonized." The award presentation was made backstage before the second-night curtain, with mock solemnity and all the cast and crew in attendance. This broke the tension, made the actor in question feel better, and boosted the energy of everyone concerned.

■ *Don't act elated when others are depressed.* Sometimes there's a tendency to make jokes and ignore the pain caused by a poor review. But remember, you're not celebrating a disaster. You want to be sympathetic and helpful. Tell your cast and crew you are proud of their achievements. Encourage them to help each other.

■ *Keep your own personal morale high.* This is most important because your company will sense your own feelings about the situation even without your saying a word. Remember that you've been doing a good job. Keep on doing it well. Let the cast know by the way you act that it is business as usual tonight, that you expect everyone to be on time with all the energy they can muster. In the end, this is the best medicine you can offer.

DIRECTING THE MUSICAL

PART VI

*M*usical theater has an immense following and brings with it special challenges for the director. In many ways, it is a hybrid, a unique theatrical form. In this section, we'll look at both the basics and some of the fine points of directing the musical.

31 | Song and Dance
The Eight Basics of Directing the Musical

Perhaps the greatest misunderstanding about musicals is that they are merely plays with music added. It's also the greatest danger, for if you believe it, you are setting yourself up for problems. In fact, the musical is its own theatrical form and demands its own directorial approach.

If you are directing a musical for the first time, or do so only occasionally, consider the following suggestions. They come from thirty years of observations as a director, performer, and student of musical theater.

Choose Carefully

If this is your first musical, consider one with the fewest technical demands, a small to medium cast, and a relatively simple structure (*Once Upon a Mattress*, for example, or *You're a Good Man, Charlie Brown*). That way you can get comfortable with the form without overtaxing yourself or your resources.

Novice or not, don't take on a show unless you genuinely like it or appreciate it. The musical is a fragile construct, and if you don't believe in the show, neither will the actors or the audience.

If you don't already have a copy, by all means get Peter Filichia's *Let's Put on a Musical!*, with much helpful information on choosing the right show for your situation.

Play to Your Strengths

Focus on what you do well and delegate the rest. Some directors are better at working with small groups or individual actors. Unfortunately, most musicals are not small. You will find much of your time may be spent working with the ensemble because it needs the most work, and in musicals the big picture is important.

If you find moving herds of people around stage is unpleasant, enlist a choreographer to help you. Even if a song isn't *choreographed* in any usual sense of the word, good stage movement is important, and most choreographers seem to thrive on working with groups. If you don't have a choreographer available, try enlisting an assistant director. Either way, this will free you to concentrate on other aspects of the show. At the very least, have someone you trust come in and view the show during rehearsal to give you some perspective on how things look.

Plan Carefully

Musicals take more organization than plays because there are more pieces involved and usually more people. On top of whatever else a play may demand, there is music to be learned and dances to be choreographed. Rehearsals will be more complicated too, because actors who have learned their music suddenly forget it when asked to dance at the same time (and vice versa).

It takes a lot longer to stage a musical number than a straight scene. More important, musical numbers take longer to say the same thing as spoken dialogue. They must sustain mood and character over a longer period of time. But unlike a play, you can't ask the actors to speed up (or slow down) the dialogue, change pitch, or turn upstage. Musicals are more apt to be presentational. Thus, staging means reblocking, adjusting the volume of singers and orchestra, and struggling with music cues.

So, plan realistically for enough rehearsal time. Unlike a play, you won't have the performers all to yourself. In most cases, a musical director will need time to work with them on songs, and a choreographer will want time to stage dance numbers.

Six weeks is a minimum rehearsal time if you rehearse five days a week; if it's your first show, add a week or two to be safe. The larger the cast or the more complex the technical demands, the longer the rehearsal period needs to be. It's better to allow too much time than too little; you'll cheer up the cast (and yourself) if you announce a night off because things are going so well.

Keep It Simple

Keep your direction simple. Fussy details impede the momentum of the well-constructed musical. As it turns out, most shows are rather simplistic in their presentation of ideas—even *Fiddler on the Roof* and *West Side Story*. That's because so much of the time is spent singing and dancing that ideas (and plot) must be presented cleanly and simply. Unfortunately, many novice directors think they have to produce flash and glitter—a parade of big production numbers that bring down the house. You'll find that you get better audience response if you parcel out the big moments so they stand out by comparison with the rest of the show.

Emphasize Character

Pay attention to character and pacing, for these are the two elements that can make or break your production.

Work with your performers to create strong characterizations. Most musicals don't spend a lot of time in developing characters; they spring fully blown, as recognizable types (and sometimes stereotypes). This is a kind of theatrical shorthand that strikes some people as shallowness, but could just as easily be called efficiency.

However, if musical-comedy characters tend to be types, they cannot be played well without empathy. One of our editors recently saw a community-theater production of *Guys and Dolls* that was excellent in almost every respect. But the director (or perhaps the actress) had misjudged Sarah Brown as being *only* prim and repressed. Certainly, the joke is that Sky Masterson must talk this reserved young woman into flying to Havana with him. But for Sky to fall in love with her, there must be some fire underneath the facade. This was missing in this actress' portrayal, leaving the audience to wonder just what Sky Masterson sees in her.

Shakespearean director Jack Lynn says he always looks for the dramatic moments in a comedy to emphasize for contrast. That way, the comedy is made even funnier.

"When I read a play for the first time, I go through it looking for places where I can ask the characters to play against the obviousness of the text. So that the thing has a dimension and can still be believable."

Thus, *Kiss Me, Kate*'s Lilli Vanessi and Fred Graham are more than merely overinflated egos. Those egos can be seen as defense mechanisms rooted in deep insecurities. We still can laugh at their excesses, but if the actors also portray the insecurities as well, we feel closer to Fred and Lilli as human beings.

Keep It Moving

Pacing is vital to the musical for several reasons. First, musicals are constructed as song-dialogue-song-dialogue. And yet, you must avoid any sense of things coming to a halt when a musical number ends—or worse, of the play coming to a halt when a song begins. Work toward a seamless flow.

Because musicals tend to be more episodic than straight plays, that flow is sometimes harder to maintain. Some shows are simply better than others in this respect. *The Unsinkable Molly Brown* is a particular problem, with scenes in widely flung locales and covering a period of many years. On the other hand, *Oklahoma!* takes place in one locale within a very short period of time.

Most musicals use the first act to introduce the characters, set up the situation, and create a conflict, with a crisis point normally placed just before the first-act curtain. The second act is normally shorter and focuses on resolving the conflict. Thus, pacing is most crucial in the first act; in most cases, the second-act momentum is built in. You'll need to work at getting the show moving from the first moment.

Avoid the Hollywood Trap

We know it's hard, but try not to let film versions scare or influence you. You're putting on a stage production, after all. Don't try to copy the film; you'll only look bad by comparison. Instead, work to create a unique look and feel your audience will appreciate on its own merits.

Happily Ever After

Musicals are fairy tales. They tell us what we want to believe—that most people are good, that bad people are punished, that life is worth living. With very few exceptions (*Evita* is one), they're supposed to send people away feeling happy, satisfied that all loose ends have been tied up. People go to musicals to be entertained. And the one great secret to a successful musical is that none of the hard work should show. The audience wants to relax and enjoy itself. If the audience senses you laboring, the illusion is destroyed. If you maintain the illusion, audience members will leave the theater feeling that you have done a good job. And they'll be right.

Get a Move On

In Musicals, Pacing Is Key

32

O ne of the most common faults in musical productions is that the pace tends to drag. The reason is simple: Three different media—speech, dance, and song—are being combined in different ways and each makes strong demands on the performers.

Assuming you have escaped the curse of the triple-threat performer—can't sing, can't dance, can't act—it's still true that a wonderful vocalist may be a poor dancer or stilted in dialogue delivery. So, how does a director work with the cast to combine the three basic elements to create an all-around entertainment?

First, know where each performer's strength lies and shape the production accordingly. For example, avoid long dance routines with inexperienced performers, especially when singing or complex action follows.

Second, try to achieve a balance in your staging so the performer's strongest area emerges as such and any weaker areas are played down. The actor who can't move and sing at the same time might be blocked to begin his song seated in a chair, then moved to a new position in the interlude between verses.

Third, identify the flagging scenes and run them as isolated sequences, simplifying where necessary and emphasizing to the cast the importance of keeping the sequence moving. It's a good idea to have three or four rehearsals set aside for fixing problems. Then, during rehearsal you can make notes of which things need work. Look particularly at your stage groupings; poor contact between performers often slows down scenes.

Last, dialogue scenes are often the weakest point of musical productions because they get too little rehearsal. It's tempting to push hardest on the musical numbers, but these do have a certain amount of momentum on their own. Once the music stops, there is nothing to drive a scene forward except the energy the actors bring to it. Be sure to schedule enough time for dialogue scenes and don't be fooled into thinking your performers are principally singers and dancers. Even if true, this is exactly why they need more, not less, dialogue work.

Step-Kick-Turn
How One Non-Choreographer Coped

STEPHEN PEITHMAN

R ecently, I agreed to direct *Tintypes*, stepping in at the last minute to replace a director/choreographer who had been chosen precisely because the show would benefit from his dance expertise. While I have directed many musicals and have created some basic stage movement in the process, I am not a choreographer.

Four of the five cast members were dancers, and three were also choreographers—a somewhat daunting situation, perhaps. As I thought about the show, the question came up: Should I allow the performers to choreograph their own numbers?

I asked this question of one of the performers, who responded, "I can choreograph other people, but I can't choreograph myself." Another said he could choreograph himself and his partner if I gave them the overall concept, while another was content to work on his own solo number only.

Given this, plus the need to get on with the rehearsals, I blocked the show, including the dance numbers, giving a strong sense of what each element was to accomplish. This allowed me, as director, to make sure every part of the show referred to my overall concept.

33

Within this framework, however, performers were free—and, as a matter of course, invited—to modify and improve what I had done. In some cases, the final choreography bore only the outline of what I had first blocked; in other cases, it was almost identical.

I surprised myself in my ability to come up with useable movement; my biggest liability was the lack of a repertory of dance styles and steps and of a vocabulary to explain the precise steps I wanted. I often had to show or describe a step I had seen others do and then ask what it was called; then a *real* dancer could demonstrate for the others. To provide the outline for what I wanted, I had to come up with some way to write down the kind of movement or effect I needed. Originally, I penciled in steps and blocking next to the lyrics in the script. Because I changed this so often as I worked before each rehearsal, the pages soon became full of indecipherable pencil marks and erasures.

My solution was to turn to my computer. In my word-processing program, I typed in all the lyrics in upper-case letters, leaving a space between each line. I then typed in blocking ideas directly below each line, only in lower-case letters. This allowed me to try things out in my head (and in my home), then redo the blocking as often as needed. I then printed out the results, put them in a three-ring binder, and took them to rehearsals. This gave me a clear view of what was going on; as we made changes in rehearsal, I penciled these in. If the changes became great, I edited the computer version and printed out new pages.

Here's an example of how this looked ("E," "T," "a," "C," and "S" refer to characters in the show).

IT'S FIFTY-FIFTY, IT'S FIFTY-FIFTY

Face out

NOT SIXTY-FORTY, NOR SEVENTY-THIRTY

E turns out R, then S turns out L

Outside shoulders should touch

I'VE FIGURED YOUR PERCENTAGE HONEY, IT WON'T DO

Point to audience on "your"

YOU'VE BEEN CHEATING ME AND I'VE BEEN SQUARE WITH YOU

Thumb on fist to chest, then point out

I'M GETTING EVEN, IT'S EVEN-STEPHEN

Move down L

I'M WISE TO YOUR LIES CAUSE YOU'VE OPENED UP MY EYES

Stop: touch L hand to R knee on "wise"

Touch R hand to L knee on "lies"

Touch L hand to R shoulder on "open"

Touch R hand to L shoulder on "up"

Both hands to face on "eyes"

For a more complex dance, I used < > marks to indicate direction of movement or the direction a performer is facing:

KEEP UP SPEED, TAKE THE LEAD, THIS IS YOUR ONLY CHANCE

Kick-walk, rotating in circle; when done, woman should be facing away from center and be downstage of man

```
Start     Finish
E> <a     T> <C
<T C>     <E a>
```

I found this approach a useful tool. Perhaps others will as well.

34 | Big Show, Small Cast

Turn a Challenge into an Advantage by Rethinking Your Artistic Concept

SCOTT MILLER

The company I work with is a small, alternative musical theater group, so we don't get the great number of people at auditions other companies might get for *Godspell* or *The Music Man*. There have been times when this has been a real problem for us, but with a production of *Pippin,* we learned this problem could be turned into an advantage.

At our auditions, only about twenty-five people showed up—some of them, frankly, not very good. Needing seven leads and a chorus for *Pippin*, I didn't know how I was going to cast the show.

I decided I needed to look at the show fresh, and forget what I knew about the Broadway production, the video version, and other productions I had seen. I had to unlearn everything I knew about doing a big musical, and ask myself some very basic questions. These were questions you might ask yourself any time you find yourself in the same situation.

First, is the musical in question "big" because the story demands it or because that's just the way everyone does it? Could the leads also be in the chorus, as with *A Chorus Line* and other concept musicals? Can we cast the same actor in more than one role without upsetting the show's premise? What would happen to the material if we did the show without a big chorus? Would that go against the creators' original intentions? And—perhaps most important—will the audience accept our choices if we don't match their preconceived notions of how this show should look?

In our case, we decided *Pippin* was a "big" musical only because that's the way most people do it. However, a closer look reveals the cast is "a group of actors," according to the stage directions. "Their costumes are of an undetermined period. But they are definitely players . . . a troupe . . . a theatrical caravan of some kind." So, it made perfect sense for our own actors to play more than one part, to appear both as a lead and in the chorus.

Using a small cast thus would remind the audience this was indeed a troupe of actors, not really Pippin's family, and that they were making this up as they went. Casting the same actor as both Charles and (in drag) his mother, Bertha, also reinforced the important concept that these people were only actors. With the major players all doubling as chorus members, we needed fewer people to fill out the cast. And it proved a lot more fun for the actors, who each now had several parts to play.

From this point, we began to explore related issues. Near the end of the play, Leading Player says to the audience, "We'll be there for you . . . waiting . . . anytime you want us. Why, we're right inside your heads." Clearly, the implication is that the Players are all in Pippin's mind—or our collective imagination. This premise gave us tremendous license; if everything in the show is an illusion, then is it possible to go too far? Treating the show as a hallucination allowed our unusual casting choices to make perfect sense.

We ended up casting only eleven actors in the show, since a *commedia dell'arte* traveling theater company probably would employ as few actors as possible and who could play many roles, in order to keep costs down. Even when two of our eleven actors dropped out because of scheduling conflicts, I found this wasn't a problem. All the performers were strong actors and singers. And because the stage we perform on is tiny, even with only nine people it still looked pretty full for the group scenes.

Most important, the show's basic premise of a traveling troupe of players playing out Pippin's life for him seemed more real because our own troupe was small, everyone doubling parts, taking walk-on parts, participating in the orgy scene, and making only minor costume changes (for instance, a hat, a tunic, a mask) to change from one character to another. The audience enjoyed the joke of the same actor playing both Pippin's father and grandmother—without Pippin noticing the resemblance!

To maintain unity in the design elements, our casting demanded that our sets likewise be minimal and extremely versatile, which forced us to be creative and also ended up saving us lots of money.

Although I'd seen *Pippin* many times and have loved the show for years, suddenly it seemed new again, without actually having changed the material at all. It wasn't the same show everyone else has done, which allowed those of us who knew the show to appreciate once again what first made us love the material. The audience, too, felt like it was seeing the show for the first time. Our reinvention impressed many people enough that they continue to attend our productions just to see how we'll approach familiar material.

I must emphasize again that our audiences accepted the show's new look because it made sense. We changed nothing simply for the sake of change. Instead, we simplified, eliminating the clutter of spectacle, allowing what we thought was the essence of the show to shine through. What we discovered could apply to dozens of other musicals. After all, at its core, the best theater isn't about crowds, special effects, or big sets. It's about people.

SPECIAL CHALLENGES

M ost directors know it is impossible to predict all the challenges a production will present. Many of the issues mentioned in the next several chapters will arise infrequently—but when they do, you'll want to know how to deal with them.

Perhaps the most complex and sensitive of those issues is how to deal with controversy. While art is, of course, expression, the expression of thoughts and feelings differs so markedly, it's no wonder controversy can emerge when plays are produced—or even considered. Is that word offensive? Is this political view a challenge to community standards? Is this scene appropriate for youngsters? In this and the next chapter, we examine some of the chief considerations a director must face when dealing with controversial material.

35 | *Staying Focused Under Fire*

Actors in a Controversial Play Need the Support of the Director

W hen an uproar arose over the Charlotte Repertory Theatre's production of *Angels in America*, it set us to wondering about its effect on the actors. How did they focus on their work while a storm of controversy raged around them? How does an actor cope with outside distractions?

As we researched the subject, however, we found the *real* story was how a director and producing company can create a safe environment in which the actors can do their best work, even under highly charged and distracting circumstances.

Creating such an environment begins with the director's concept and staging, then flourishes with solid company support and effective communication with the audience and the community at large.

Let the Work Speak

Some plays are born controversial and some have controversy thrust upon them. However, in either case, it's important to remember the controversy is *not* the play.

"You pick a play first because it makes good theater," says Bruce Tinker, managing artistic director of North Dakota's Fargo-Moorhead Community Theater. "But I think some directors tend to pounce on the controversy. They beat people over the head with it, rather than just tell the story. It may even be a personal agenda item: They *want* to confront the audience. But if the play is well crafted, the confrontation, if any, is built in. My suggestion is to let the work speak for itself."

Director/actor James Carver, formerly of Michigan's Kalamazoo Civic Players, agrees, adding that most companies have to "work within the mores of the society that surrounds them. You can push, you can get the audience to accept more and more. But there are certain limits, particularly in community theater. Touring companies can do a lot more daring things than a group in which the director and actors have to deal with bosses, friends, and family."

If a company has picked a controversial work it believes has something of value to offer the audience, then it becomes a question of finding a way to make it emotionally and intellectually accessible to that audience—to those bosses, friends, and family who surround the actors. One way is through creative staging.

"There's a way to deal with profanity or nudity," Carver says. "For example, through blocking, you can change the focus so it's not as confrontational. As directors, we do this all the time, anyway—we shift focus onstage for any number of reasons."

Of course, you need to ask yourself how much softening you can do without harming the play. And, in the end, you may not be able to soften things enough to suit everyone, anyway.

"We all hate criticism, but sometimes you just have to bite the bullet," says Michael Fortner, executive director of Theatre Memphis. "You know you'll get flack, but you have to believe in the shows you do."

Get the Word Out

When you know the show you're producing will be highly controversial to a significant number of people, the best thing you can do is warn them of what they're going to see, Fortner advises.

"Make it clear what it's about, the language, the situations. That way, the audience will air its grievances early, and you can address these questions more easily when the pressure isn't on. Write it into your marketing materials. This is critical, because once your audience knows you are going to be straight with them, they will trust you about your choices.

"The worst thing is when the audience is not prepared for what they're about to see," Fortner adds. "That's when you get comments like, 'I'm shocked. I paid good money for a ticket and you didn't tell me what I'd be seeing or hearing. I brought my thirteen-year-old daughter and I was embarrassed.' That is simply poor public relations and doesn't do anything to build an audience for your theater. An honest communication policy is best."

Bruce Tinker also believes preparing the audience should begin with the first point of communication with it.

"From the moment they first hear about the play to the moment they sit down in their seat to watch the show, it's all part of the theater experience. And it's part of our job to create a positive experience. It starts with the way the theater company is presented to the community, the way shows are advertised. A lot of it is audience trust, that if you do something outside their normal ken, they will trust your choice."

A Model of Preparedness

It's instructive to see the preparation made by Charlotte Repertory for its production of *Angels in America*. First, all advertising for the play contained a warning about the show's adult language, graphic scenes, and nudity. The warning also was posted at the box office and theater, and was included in the direct-mail campaign and in all ticket envelopes. The company recommended the show for people eighteen years old and over, and group sales were prohibited for schools below the college or university level.

As the opening drew nearer and the controversy heated up, the theater company distributed a fact sheet to patrons, community groups, and the press. It included answers to such questions as "Why is Charlotte Rep doing a show like *Angels in America*?," "Why is Charlotte Rep doing a show about homosexuals?," and "Why is this play so graphic?"

Keith Martin, Charlotte Rep's managing director, arranged a series of educational forums, including a conversation with playwright Tony Kushner and a discussion of the play's spiritual themes led by members of Charlotte's religious community.

"This isn't just a performance," Martin told the *Charlotte Observer*. "This is an entire series of educational and outreach programs."

Support Is Key

Among the earliest converts were the nonprofit theater's board of trustees.

"Knowing the board was totally behind us made a difference," says *Angels* actor Mary Lucy Bivens. "So did Keith's coming to us, reassuring us that everything was being taken care of. We were very well insulated. There was great effort to keep us in an environment where we could stay focused."

Keeping the actors away from the limelight was a conscious decision, says director Steve Umberger, again in an effort to put the focus on the play. It wasn't easy.

"There were security guards around the theater," Bivens recalls. "There was uncertainty about safety, of course, but we also had newspeople trying to slip through the loading dock."

"We did no media interviews with the cast and me," Umberger explains. "We left the media to Keith. Many national television shows wanted to do features. One wanted to tape the disrobing scene, then alter it electronically to hide the nudity. I said no, absolutely not. That would only focus attention on what really is a fleeting moment in the play, important as it is. And Keith backed me up."

Bruce Tinker points out that actors are already somewhat cut off from the rest of the community, and sometimes that can be troublesome.

"One problem is the rehearsal period is somewhat insular," he says. "You become so familiar with the material, you don't even think of its effect on others. You develop relationships that don't include a lot of outside folks. And all of a sudden it's externalized in performance and you get feedback for which you're not prepared."

On with the Show

On opening night of *Angels*, Mary Lucy Bivens says her biggest concern was " 'What happens if the show goes on and the opposing forces buy tickets and disrupt the performance?' Fortunately, we knew the people who were working behind the scenes would take care of us if this happened. It didn't."

Letters of support were posted backstage, including one from playwright Tony Kushner that read, in part, "Trust in the play and your own artistry," and others from Actor's Equity, Dramatists Play Service (*Angels* is not one of its plays), and the North Carolina Theatre Conference.

Support was evident in the theater as well. Before opening-night curtain, Keith Martin spoke to the audience, saying simply, "Welcome to *Angels in America*."

"There was thunderous applause," recalls Bivens, who was waiting to make her entrance. "The audience jumped to their feet and roared. Then Keith introduced Tony Kushner, which brought another roar. There was so much energy, so much electricity. It infused the entire performance."

Doing the Right Thing

Just as the director should think through the play and its impact before beginning rehearsal, it is equally important to restate to the cast and crew the strength of your work and the rightness of the choice. This is particularly so if there is significant opposition to the production. In those cases, James Carver believes the director should call everyone for a brief discussion.

"We do it when a show gets a bad review," he says, "and for the same reason. You want to acknowledge the actors' feelings, their anger, and you want to redirect their focus back to the play. You have to help them understand that one comment, or several angry letters, must not change the trust you've built up that what you're doing is right. You need to tell them you have achieved what you set out to achieve."

As for audience members walking out of a performance, Carver tells his cast, 'There are a lot of people who aren't going to like what's going on. They're going to be offended by it. They don't like the message or they don't like the language. But there are a lot of people who need to hear this message. And, after all, we *are* exploring the human condition. It may be some people can't take the human condition and they need to get up and leave because they don't like to see it portrayed for them. They would rather believe that doesn't exist."

That was made clear when *Angels in America* actor Alan Poindexter was asked why he didn't avoid the furor by simply standing sideways or hiding his genitals. He responded: "Because the character [an AIDS patient] is being examined by a nurse. He is at the most vulnerable, stripped-down point in his life."

Actors in a controversial show or playing disreputable characters also may be at their most vulnerable. It's up to the director and the entire company to help protect them.

You Want to Do a Play About WHAT?

A Firsthand Experience in High School Theater

JEROME MCDONOUGH

36

Sex education.

No two words have caused more of an uproar in American education than these two. As a result, many prospective directors of high school theater may be hesitant to even consider a play like *Dolls*, fearing comments such as "Too explicit," "Too controversial," "We don't have a problem with that here," or "It will give them ideas!"

Let's not kid ourselves. With the possible exception of communities that still lack electricity, sex is heard about on the radio; viewed on television soap operas, videos, and commercials; discussed in every gathering of more than one teenager; and engaged in—according to recent surveys—by fully half of our young people by the time they complete high school—those who complete high school.

If they get ideas from this play, the ideas won't be new ones. Actually, the groups of people who would like to see such a play produced may surprise you. People like many religious leaders. People like the medical community in your city. People like most of the parents of the teens and preteens in your school system.

"But how do I even broach the subject with my community?" I hear you ask. The best course is to be certain nobody gets surprised by the play.

1. Tell your administrators and counselors you would like to perform the play and provide scripts for them to read. Tough as it might be, set a time frame to check back with them. If, after reading the script, they are still reluctant to do the show, try to get them to at least agree to let you pursue the next step. (Step 2 is necessary, regardless.)

2. Meet with the parents of prospective cast members and send scripts home with them so they will know what to expect. Give the parents a form so they can express their opinion. The original production of my plays *Juvie* and *Addict*, as well as *Dolls,* followed this procedure. I have yet to receive my first dissenting vote from a parent on these scripts. Frequently, encouraging notes were attached to the approval slip. Such parental endorsement should convince your administrators to let you proceed.

3. Once the permission slips are in, cast the show and go on with the preparation of the play.

4. Present a couple of closed preview performances for the parents of the community and your school's teachers and staff. This step is particularly important if the play is to be presented at school during the school day. If some parents object to the show, they can request that their children not attend the performance. If production plans include touring to other campuses, invite the parents, teachers, and administrators of those schools to the previews. Mount a big publicity campaign for those performances.

5. Once everything is a go, present the play to every audience you can reach. Each community will have to decide at which grade level attendance for a play like *Dolls* should start. Seventh grade seems about right. Younger students may be aware to a degree, but a bit more sophisticated knowledge of dating, social pressures, the mechanics of sex, and boy-girl relationships is required before the play will be meaningful. (Different tools are more appropriate at lower grade levels . . . and are desperately needed.)

Hold for Laughter

Effective Comedy Needs Work to Seem Effortless

37

NANCIANNE PFISTER

"Dying is easy. Comedy is difficult."

So, the story goes, said actor Edmund Gwenn on his deathbed (although the quote often is erroneously ascribed to Edmund Kean). James Carver, former director of Michigan's Kalamazoo Civic Theatre, is fond of quoting Gwenn. He believes it underscores essential differences between comedy and drama as they function for the audience.

"In comedy, timing is everything. That timing can't always be taught, but rather depends on the sensitivity of the actor. Unlike drama, comedy doesn't give the audience time to think. Even the function of a pause is different. A dramatic pause pulls us into the scene; in comedy, a pause allows the audience to go ahead of you and sets up the gag."

We were fortunate to attend Carver's workshop on how to direct comedy (sponsored by the American Association of Community Theatre). His comments were specific and useful, reflecting his many years of experience in the theater. And they point out the essential role of the director in making a comedy funny to the audience.

The director's first task, Carver says, is to locate the

comedic elements in the script. Does the comedy come from ordinary people in extraordinary circumstances or does it come from characters so odd that any situation in which they are involved is funny?

To aid this process, Carver cites five key elements that make us laugh.

1. *Identification with the characters.* When we recognize ourselves in the words and actions of the players, we also have a sense of relief that says, "It's not just me." Many *Seinfeld* scripts, for example, involve obsession with the picky details of life. Carver also offers as an example someone who goes to the movies and worries about which armrest is his. This is a silly concern, but most of us have experienced it, so we laugh at the character who shares our concern.

2. *Feeling superior to the characters.* Sometimes the audience knows something the character has yet to discover. We laugh because we know the results of an action the character cannot foresee. At other times, our feeling of superiority comes from believing we would never act as foolishly as the character. In the final scene of *Morning's at Seven,* for example, Arry enters wearing gloves and a hat and carrying suitcases. She is moving out of her sister's house. In response to a question about her destination, she says, "I'm moving over to Ida's." Ida is another sister who lives *next door*. We would never don traveling clothes to move next door, and we laugh at her pretension.

3. *Unexpected physical acts.* Anyone who's ever seen a Marx Brothers' movie or a French farce knows how much laughter can be provoked by a lot of people rushing about, slamming doors. In a classic *Three Stooges* piece, Larry, Curly, and Moe are making a birthday cake. We laugh at their sloppy measuring, impossible ingredients, and complete disregard for directions. (Conversely, we laugh at their "exact" following of directions, such as dropping three eggs into the batter without removing the shells.) When the batter, now the texture of Silly Putty, is finally in the oven, we speculate on the outcome. Will the cake explode? Will it swell so much it bursts the door of the oven? Will it produce enough smoke to bring the fire department, thereby setting up a round of antics with hoses and ladders? When the Stooges remove the cake from the oven, however, not only is it perfectly baked, it is frosted, decorated, and has candles burning on it. This is the last thing we expect, so we laugh.

4. *Unexpected word combinations* make us laugh, as do shifts in points of view. Parodies rely on this. Take something familiar out of

context and the audience, made aware of a new meaning for the same words, will laugh. One of the most quoted lines from *Casablanca* is Rick's toast; he raises a glass to Ilse and says, "Here's looking at you, Kid." In a Gilbert and Sullivan-style parody, *The Pirates of Casablanca,* Rick delivers the line after raising a telescope and training it on Ilse, barely fifteen feet away. He is now literally "looking at you," and absurdly so, and the audience laughs.

5. *Repetition*. The running gag is a well-known comedy device (for example, the old man making the seven circuits around the walls of Rome in *A Funny Thing Happened on the Way to the Forum*). So is a departure from expected repetition or a break in the rhythms that have been established. For example, if each time someone opens a door, the knob comes off in his hand, we laugh. But what happens later when the actor approaches the door cautiously but the knob does not come off? We laugh because he (and we) have been fooled. We laugh even more if the actor, *needing* the repetition, pulls and twists until the knob is forced off and he can shoot a glance of triumph at the audience. He has conquered the knob! The fact that he has conquered it to his own inconvenience makes it silly, and we laugh.

Making It Happen

As these elements suggest, there is a consistent technique for getting laughs from a particular play.

"Don't let a single comic moment pass you by, then help the audience get the laughs," Carver says. "Give them permission to laugh by holding for laughter and by letting them know early on what they're in for. In the first few moments, the audience is gathering information, looking at the scenery and costumes. Create a comic moment as soon as you can."

Carver believes comedy is technical, that the actor always must be in control, aware of the rhythms of a play. No matter how silly the words or the actions, the characters must take seriously everything that happens or the audience won't buy it. Nothing kills comedy more than an actor who, out of character, indicates "Aren't I *funny?*"

Carver offers several cautions aimed at helping audiences get all the laughs the director intended.

1. *Beware the split focus.* "The audience should focus on the face of the actor," Carver says. "The audience must see the setup. If there is action elsewhere on the stage, the comic line can be lost."

At the end of *Twelfth Night,* Olivia sees her twin and everything becomes clear to her. She expresses her understanding in just two words, "Most wonderful!" The line can be blurred by other action on stage or it can stand alone, gathering total focus so the audience is moved to laughter and applause.

2. *Trust your first instincts.* "Don't add physical stuff at the end of rehearsal time, when you're used to the script and it's no longer funny to you. The things that made you laugh the first time you read the script will make the audience laugh the first time, too. If you add last-minute stuff, you may steal focus."

3. *Raise the comfort level.* Making a comparison with animated cartoons, Carver notes that an audience worried about the characters is unlikely to laugh.

"Particularly in physical comedy, the audience has to know the characters are not in danger. Look at Road Runner cartoons. When the rock falls on Wile E. Coyote, we know he's not dead; that wouldn't be funny. In *Noises Off,* a character falls down the stairs. If he lay there and someone else had the next line, the audience would worry. By giving him the line immediately after his fall, the audience is relieved he is OK, and they can laugh."

4. *Timing is everything.* Carver believes there are two paces in comedy—"Fast and faster. You need to vary the timing so you can deliver the unexpected payoff. The line length is your clue to the pace of the scene. Long speeches are fast; short speeches are faster."

All this sounds like much work for actors and directors, but Carver insists that following these points is what's really important. *Too much* effort cuts down on the audience's enjoyment.

"You never want an audience to sense you are working. When you are working too hard, it just doesn't happen. It's got to seem easy."

Who's in Charge Here?

Codirecting Challenges Two Leaders to Share a Vision—Here's How to Make It Work

"**W**hen we work together, once it's done, [I think] everything was *my* idea."

Ivan Sandoval is describing successful sharing of directing chores with producer John Beaudry. He must know something, because the team has directed such works as *Equus, A Man for All Seasons, Who's Afraid of Virginia Woolf?,* and *A Walk in the Woods.*

Beaudry agrees with Sandoval that the final presentation should be so seamless that it is impossible even for the directors to say which of them was responsible for individual production elements.

"It's crucial you don't care whose idea it was. It doesn't matter if we know what we're after. The only thing we care about is making the show work."

Many (perhaps most) people assume a show's director has the same authority as a ship's captain, so it might seem unlikely anyone would agree to do it except in an emergency. (*Stage Directions* editor Stephen Peithman admits to being enough of a "control freak" that he finds it difficult sharing directorial responsibility with another person. Many of our readers share his view, but others, like Sandoval and Beaudry, do not.)

Obviously, the system works for some, and we wanted to know more: How do codirectors divide the work load and how do actors respond to having more than one person in charge? We also sought advice on choosing a compatible codirector, for if there was one overwhelming point of agreement, it was that not just anyone will do.

A Choice, Not a Need

"Bev and I didn't *need* to work together; we *chose* to work together," says Jeanne Stein of her collaboration with Beverly Wallwork at Los Alamos Little Theatre in New Mexico. Each of the long-standing friends also had directed the other. "We are not afraid to say what we think," says Stein. "We are not afraid to listen; we are not afraid to decide."

"We're friends," repeats Wallwork, "so we could cope. We were both interested in the play, *The Boys Next Door.* Codirecting is not my first choice, but it's great if you don't have all the time and energy needed to devote to a show."

Patti L'Italien and Candy Cleland of Stage Left Players in Salem, Ohio, also had worked under each other's direction before combining directorial talents for *Hail to the Chef.* "Even though we tend to look at things differently, we're comfortable giving criticism," says L'Italien. "You have to be flexible, with no big ego, or it can't work."

Stein supports the notion of flexibility. "You have to use whatever works; you can't think of change as a negative thing. This is a learning experience. The more input, the more you learn."

That view is shared by Elaine Edstrom, formerly of California's Woodland Opera House, who advises that directors not "agree to do this without knowing you have the same vision of the show and can agree on the casting," recalling a graduate-school collaboration that was "the worst."

"I was assigned to codirect with my graduate advisor. I was close to his age—older than most students—and had experience directing in professional theater," she says. "It didn't matter; he disagreed with every idea I had. I needed the experience to get my degree, so there was nothing I could say."

Edstrom thinks women may be more amenable to the notion of codirecting and offers a feminist perspective.

"It's been a long, hard road for women to be taken seriously as directors. Think back forty years. All the directors, all the designers were men. Women have made their mark working with each other."

Working Methods

Sometimes, of course, directors don't see eye to eye. What then?

"If we haven't agreed on what the play is about, as articulated in the text, I'll direct one show, John will direct another," says Sandoval. "We spend as much time talking about this as we do in rehearsal. If either of us thought he wasn't a part of it, it wouldn't happen."

For those who do choose to direct with a partner, the earliest decisions revolve around casting and the subsequent division of labor.

"We did the casting together," says L'Italien. "They were all well-seasoned actors so we knew how they worked. None of them were unfamiliar to us. I'm better at the mechanical side of things, so I did the rough blocking. Candy has a more personal style. She did the fine-tuning and characterization. She was good at getting a little more out of the actors than they thought they could give."

The Beaudry-Sandoval team has several working methods, depending on the show, the cast, and the time available. As the company's producer, Beaudry often has played devil's advocate to Sandoval's solo directing. As partners, one may work with all the major characters, leaving the other to direct the ensemble. Or one will act as observer for the other, commenting on how close the blocking comes to the vision they share.

"Sometimes," says Sandoval, "I will do the blocking until I feel something isn't working. Then I turn to John and say, 'How are you going to solve this?' "

Edstrom also has split directing chores between major and minor characters. Whether codirecting or working with an assistant, she thinks it's good "to have that second pair of eyes, someone to say 'This is what *I* see.' "

That second pair of eyes can come in handy from the outset. Wallwork says she and Stein make casting decisions in tandem. "Normally, we don't have huge turnouts for auditions. We have to fit people into the characters. In our company, the director is responsible for getting the technical staff. We struggle to get builders and designers."

"Bev has a fine eye for design," explains Stein. "She did the staging; I did the directing, but Bev also worked with the actors. We think the same way. Someone asked if it might not be better if we did not. I don't think so."

A Matter of Control

Colleen Parker of Pike County Little Theatre in Mississippi isn't buying any of this, in spite of a successful, though unplanned, directorial partnership. Parker was working with an apprentice director on *The Good Doctor* when she had to leave the show for emergency surgery. The apprentice took over with good results. Even so, Parker rejects the codirector concept.

"There's only room for one director; you can't have two captains on the ship. In a musical, there are lots of directors: a musical director, a vocal director, and a choreographer. You want to respect all of them, but they know you have the final word.

"A friend has produced several shows with me. We talk things out, but she doesn't tell me how to direct. It's a benevolent dictatorship; someone has to be in charge."

This is a matter of logistics, not ego, according to Parker, who reminds us, "A confident director won't be intimidated by a suggestion, no matter where it comes from."

The logistics problem seemed solved in a case recalled by Edstrom, but one that led to its own problems.

"I once was hired to direct a one-act play that was part of a double bill," she says. "It seemed simple enough: 'You do one; I'll do the other.' Nothing jelled."

None of the directors we talked with wanted to work by dividing scenes or acts between them. Working separately only paves the way to real problems, as Stein recalls.

"Once I had to leave a show for a while and I asked a friend to take over for me. He changed many things I had done. When I returned, I changed them back."

Although she tells the story with no rancor in her voice, Stein must have found it trying. We can only imagine how burdensome it was for the actors.

What About the Actors?

How well does the cast accept a pair of directors? Or, as Parker asked when citing her reluctance to codirect, "How do you say one has more power? To whom does the cast listen?"

"Actors can get frustrated when there are two directors," admits L'Italien. "They want to know who's in charge. The advantage of having two of us was that they were almost never frustrated with both of us at the same time."

The secret to a successful collaboration is to "let the actors know the two of you share the big picture."

Cleland agrees. "We worked well together because we never disagreed on the final product. The difference was in methodology. Patti is creative and quiet," Cleland explains. "She let the cast be almost improvisational. When I came with specific directions, the actors were frustrated. Even though I'd been around from the beginning, what I was doing was new to them. If they took my direction, they felt disloyal to Patti and looked to her for support. Once they knew we saw the same show, they were cooperative. And we always compared our rehearsal notes *before* we talked to the cast."

Having two points of view can be a positive force, Sandoval points out.

"When there are codirectors, there are two perspectives of the same event," he explains, adding it is "the joy of the actor" to reconcile those differences, since—as in real life—there is more than one way to view any situation.

"Directors need to have faced their issues or the actors will be confused," Sandoval adds. "Our actors can't get away with pitting one director against the other. When there is a question, we talk it out *while the actor is standing there listening* so there is no question about why we made the decision. That 'why' is more important than the physical action."

"People think this is magic," says Beaudry, "but it's very specific. Our combined perspective makes us understood."

39 | When You're Asked to Take Over a Show

Take a Deep Breath and Plunge In—After You've Thought It Through

A director takes sick, drops out, or is let go. Whatever the reason, you have been asked to step in and direct a show at the last minute. You feel comfortable with the show and with the rehearsal schedule, so you say yes. Now, what steps can you take to do your best work—and make the show a success? Here are some suggestions.

1. Phone the cast—at least the principals, if it's a very large show—and explain how much you're looking forward to working with them. Since you didn't choose them for the parts, they will appreciate this reassurance. By stressing how much you'll need their cooperation, you'll also cement the bond between you and them.

2. Next, phone each of the designers and managers and assure them of the same. Call a production meeting immediately to check progress on scenic, lighting, and costume design. If these have begun already, you will need to work your blocking around what is done. Don't ask for major revisions if substantial work has been completed. However, you might ask if a predominant color can be altered without

affecting lights and costumes, or if a set piece can be moved or made larger.

3. Familiarize yourself with the play by reading it through several times quickly; then several more times slowly. Pay special attention to entrances and exits; lighting cues; and interaction with sets, costumes, lights, and props. Then read the play "backwards"—that is, read the last scene, then the scene before it, and so on. This helps you understand the transitions better and gives you a grasp of how to move the play forward.

4. If it's a musical, get a copy of the recording and make a tape. If it's not a musical, make a tape of the dialogue, complete with stage directions. If you have a tape player in your car, play it when you drive to work. Play it on a Walkman-type player whenever you can. Visualize movement as you listen. Jot down any ideas.

5. If blocking already has begun, ask to see what has been accomplished. Try to work with what has been set; it will reduce your load and the stress on the actors. If anyone says, "But Joe wanted us to . . . ," just say, "I know. But I want to try it this way. If it doesn't work, we'll go back to the old way."

6. If the former director was let go or dropped out under unpleasant circumstances, don't badmouth him or her or allow anyone else to do so. Keep attention focused on the production at hand.

7. Act decisively. The cast and production staff will be reassured if you act with confidence. This does not mean you should pretend to know all the answers; rather, show you have a vision of the show you want and can articulate that vision.

8. Ask for help. In your phone calls to the cast and staff, you will have asked for their support. Now, reinforce that with a willingness to accept ideas that support your concept of the production. Make this a team effort. You are still the captain, but you'll find your task easier with everyone rowing the boat in the same direction.

9. Praise where praise is due and do so publicly.

10. Enjoy yourself. Taking over a show can be stressful. Don't let yourself get wrapped up in saving the situation. Allow yourself moments to step away from the production, to clear your head, and to rest. You'll be no good to anyone otherwise.

40 | The Student Director

Lead a Little, Lead a Lot— Which Works Best?

*T*o what extent can high school students become involved in productions? Answers vary, depending on the pool of available directing talent, the number of productions scheduled, and the time and resources available. Although some high school teachers find that students do well as directors, we like the approach followed by Margaret McClatchy, of Shawnee Mission North High School, in Overland Park, Kansas.

"Directing can be a valuable experience for selected, advanced students, but it's rare to find high school students with the necessary knowledge and experience, as well as people skills, to direct their peers," she says. She makes a good point. While it's true we often learn best by doing, the teacher has to strike a balance here. After all, the students being directed deserve a high-quality learning experience as well. It would not be fair to them if the student director is not up to the task. If either the student actor or student director does not benefit from their work together, something important is lost.

It's our experience that the term *student director* is used rather loosely, in some cases denoting an assistant to the director; McClatchy agrees.

"Unless a student supervises or assists with casting and blocking, and gives notes, I would not use the term *student director*," she says. And most high school drama teachers probably would not offer that kind of control and responsibility to a student, at least for full-scale productions. However, many—including McClatchy—do give students the opportunity to direct on a small scale, as well as taking on other major responsibilities.

"While we do not use student directors for our main productions, students whose script is chosen for our program of original one-acts may direct their script under close professional supervision," she says. "The playwrights also select their own stage manager and assistant stage manager." Seniors in McClatchy's Advanced Repertory Theatre class direct the sketches they write for their comedy shows. Students also go regularly to middle and grade schools to direct workshops or assist with play direction there.

"For our musical, a student serves as production manager and holds weekly meetings with crew heads to troubleshoot, communicate, and solve problems for the director and technical director," she explains. "We also use experienced seniors and juniors as stage managers and assistant stage managers. They have authority and status—assisting with casting, leading warm-ups, following the prompt book, recording all blocking changes, calling cues, running props and shifts."

However you choose to use students, the responsibility you give them should not exceed their ability to do a good job. However, making that call is what an instructor always does. As with any teaching experience, it comes down to a balance between giving them the freedom to learn while maintaining enough control to keep them on the right track.

41

Putting on the Dog

Canine Actors Can Be a Joy—If You Know How to Select and Direct Them

MARY JOHNSON

After deciding to put on a popular musical like *Annie* or *The Wizard of Oz*, many directors wring their hands and cry, "But what will we do about the dog?"

Everyone has heard the stories (which range from horror-filled to humorous) about working with animals: They steal the show, they bite, they lick their privates during dramatic moments. While I know of only two absolutely fool-proof solutions—an actor in a dog suit and a toy called "Go Go, My Walking Pup"—it *is* possible to find a real live animal to play the role that won't wreak havoc on your theater. In fact, with planning, patience, and teamwork, you actually may enjoy watching a wonderful relationship develop between Annie or Dorothy and her canine companion. That love will shine through on stage, adding an extra dimension to your show.

Professional or Amateur?

Your budget probably will determine whether or not you can afford to hire a professional animal actor.

Usually, the professional route creates the fewest headaches. The animal will arrive at rehearsal complete with a trainer or handler who is adept at working with actors and animals. The dog already will be trained and socialized, and the handler will teach the actors how to work with the dog to achieve the best results. Professional animal actors are generally accustomed to working around scenery, orchestras, and actors, and can be trusted to be gentle and calm under stress.

Most specialized theatrical trainers are located in major metropolitan areas, but they usually are willing to travel. Fees vary greatly, but expect to pay anywhere from $500 to $1,500 a week, plus a per diem to cover the handler's lodging, food, and travel if they're from out of town.

This may seem pricey, but a local pet supply store, underground fence company, or veterinarian may be willing to sponsor the "star" in order to share in the publicity and advertising for your show.

If your budget won't allow you to hire a professional, don't fret. It's still possible to cast a dog for the role. Your primary goal is to find a friendly, well-socialized dog who gets along well with people. Looks and previous training should be secondary to the dog's personality. The dog who excels in the theater is a laid-back animal who takes noise and commotion in stride.

If you have to choose between a dog that barks, jumps up on you, and wags its tail furiously, and another which wags politely but remains seated or standing while you meet, choose the latter.

Where to Look

When looking for a dog in your community, try contacting local dog trainers. They may have a dog that will fit the bill or they may be able to put you in touch with a client who does. Like theatrical trainers, local trainers may want a fee if they are to oversee the project from start to finish. But because they are based in your town, they also may be interested in bartering services for advertising space, access to your mailing list, or a set of season tickets. You never know until you ask.

Avoid trainers who subscribe to questionable training techniques, such as excessive collar yanking, screaming, or hitting the animal. Negative trainers have no business in show business. Work with a trainer or handler who uses positive training methods and who is willing to spend a good deal of time helping the animal become fully integrated into the performance. A dog trained in this manner will wag its tail and show its happiness.

Unless trainers have been active in the theater previously, you will need to help them understand the special needs of animal actors. I have seen dogs who excel in the show or obedience ring fall apart when placed on stage. That's because many dogs who excel at specialty dog events have exuberant personalities.

The quieter, calmer dogs tend to work better in the theater because the backstage area of a big musical is full of diversions: moving scenery, a live orchestra, and nervous actors. All can be stressful, and the pressure can be too great for many dogs, regardless of their training. Add to this the fact that the dog is expected to obey a virtual stranger (who may be a child), while the owner/handler is watching in the wings.

That's why it's important to invite trainers to spend some time backstage, so they'll understand your needs. Also, encourage the trainer and the dog to attend most, if not all, the rehearsals. Then make extra sure they don't end up idle! Schedule time for Annie or Dorothy to play and work with the dog.

Picking the Right Dog

Casting a dog from a cattle call (so to speak) makes for great press, but can leave you without a dog at the end of the day. For best results, do some homework first, so you'll have a back-up in case the dogs you audition don't work out.

Publicize your audition well; post notices at dog training schools, veterinarians' offices, pet shops, libraries, and anywhere dog lovers might hang out. Call the local papers and encourage them to cover the event. For best results, include a phone number in your advertisements, and schedule each dog for an individual five- or ten-minute appointment. Nothing is worse than having 20 to 30 dogs, some nice, and some not so nice, waiting for you in one room.

For everyone's safety and sanity, screen the dogs individually. Ask a few company members and perhaps a local dog trainer to be on hand to help in the screening. Play games, then pet the dog quietly. Make animated noises and see what the reaction is. If the owner claims the dog is obedience-trained, ask for a demonstration of the dog's skills. In the end, pick a friendly, quiet dog who is good with adults and kids and willing to listen to anyone.

Don't get too wrapped up with looks. Hollywood and Broadway have shaped our ideas of what Toto and Sandy should look like, but don't be too concerned if you head in the opposite direction. MGM did just that when they cast Toto in *The Wizard of Oz*. L. Frank Baum had a Scottish Terrier in mind when he wrote the books, but every

Scottie interviewed was either high-strung or otherwise unsuitable. They chose an experienced animal actor, who just happened to be a Cairn Terrier. Your perfect Toto may be a small mixed breed or a white bichon. Cast whichever dog has the ability and willingness to work, regardless of its looks.

Rehearsals and Performances

Once you've found the perfect dog, it's easy to keep rehearsals flowing. Follow the lead of Bill Berloni, Broadway's leading animal trainer, and make sure the dog has a handler. Appoint one member of the crew to this job. This person will make sure the dog gets to and from rehearsals safely and on time, unless the professional trainer has taken charge already. The handler also should be an advocate for the dog, and should politely remind the director when the animal's been left off the rehearsal schedule. Choose a person who loves animals, and, if possible, understands a bit about dog training.

With a local dog, the owner or trainer may want to perform this role. If that's the case, appoint an assistant handler who has worked at the theater before. People who don't routinely work in the theater often think it's a glamorous job and are disappointed when they learn how hard they must work. An assistant who understands your theater can run interference, and help keep the dog and trainer happy.

By allowing plenty of time for rehearsal, you increase your chances that the dog will settle into its role. Conversely, if you wait until tech week to integrate a dog into the show, you're going to have problems. Help the dog feel comfortable on stage and backstage by spending time with it daily, especially during the relatively calm early days of rehearsal. These work/play sessions should begin with the dog and the actress in the Annie or Dorothy role playing games, such as fetch and hide-and-seek; this will help develop the bond between human and animal.

Then carefully block and rehearse each scene. Dogs respond to repetition; the more times you can rehearse, the better the performance will be. Also, encourage the entire cast to be welcoming. They should greet the dog during each rehearsal, and take the time to get to know it a little bit. This helps the dog feel welcome and secure.

The Hooverville scene in *Annie* can be frightening for the dog unless it understands that all of those people (including the police officers) are its friends and they are all just playing at being angry and mean. Making each scene into a little game for the dog helps it feel safe and stay interested.

If you rehearse off-sight, arrange field trips to the theater for the dog and the actress so they can get used to the theater space together. If you have another show running, allow the pair to remain backstage for several nights. This will encourage the actress to accept her responsibility for the dog, and will help the dog get used to the roar of applause, the bright lights, and the moving scenery.

Obviously, socialization is the key. Keeping the dog calm, safe, and happy throughout the process should take precedence over any specific trick. Most likely, the dog you choose already knows the basic obedience commands. In that case, the actress playing Annie or Dorothy need only learn the commands and practice often for everything to fall into place. The actress will be responsible for the dog while it is performing, and the handler will be just off stage to coordinate entrances and exits, and to return the dog to its dressing room.

If your dog is not trained, and you have sufficient time, visit your local library and read one of the many dog training books available. This will give you the information you need to teach a dog to sit, stay, come, and heel.

If you've had trouble finding a dog, have very little time to prepare, or realize the dog you have isn't quite perfect, it may be wiser to cut the dog from a few scenes or put him on a leash some or all of the time. It's far better for audiences to see the dog in one scene that the animal knows very well than in many where it is out of control.

If you're doing *The Wizard of Oz*, for instance, you can adopt the strategy used in *The Wiz:* Toto does not travel to Oz and only appears in the first and last scenes of the show, set in Kansas. In *Annie*, Sandy's big walk across stage at the end of the musical number "NYC" easily can be cut, and Annie can walk into the wings to get Sandy when she first finds him.

Keep It Safe

Safety should be your prime concern. Rather than risk an injury to anyone, make changes so the dog, and actors, feel safe.

Once you've moved into the theater, take a close look around to remove any poisons or hazards. Many theaters use rat poison, which can be deadly. Keep the name of a 24-hour veterinary clinic posted on the callboard, just in case, and give the dog its own space, preferably a dressing room, classroom, or other small room, so the handler and the dog can spend time alone.

You'd be surprised at how many people will approach a strange dog because they know it's an animal actor. This can be very distracting for a well-behaved dog, and potentially dangerous if the dog is not perfectly trained. Even a well-meaning dog can jump up on a child, causing a fall.

Insist these three rules be followed:

1. Everyone should greet and pet the dog at each rehearsal.

2. No one should approach or distract the dog when he is working.

3. No one should feed or give commands to the dog (except, of course, those who need to on stage).

One last tip. Ask the owners of the dog to withhold its food during the day and require the handler to walk the dog before the performance begins. Withholding food will not hurt the dog, and makes it less likely to do something embarrassing on stage. The dog should have water available in its dressing room at all times.

If you take the time to find the right dog, socialize it with the actors and the theater, then practice often, you should have a successful run. Working with animals can be very rewarding; if done correctly, the true love between Annie and Sandy or Dorothy and Toto will shine through, and no one will notice if the dog remains standing when it should be sitting.

42 Let the Good Crimes Roll

An Interactive Murder Mystery Requires Preparation and Planning

LORI MYERS

D irecting an interactive murder mystery is very different from directing a traditional thriller. Instead of a proscenium or thrust configuration, your stage is now a dining room, the script merely a guide, and you may find your actors a bit reticent about doing improvisation and coming face-to-face (literally) with their audience.

These differences don't have to be obstacles, however. When it comes to directing an audience-participation murder mystery, you don't have to be clueless. All you need is organization, flexibility, and creativity. Here's how you can meet each of the major challenges.

By way of an example, let's say you've written an improvisational script containing funny stock characters, intrigue, and a crime. Actors are cast, costumes are ordered, props are gathered. And a local restaurant has agreed to host you.

The Space

Although Shakespeare wrote, "All the world's a stage," it will be up to you to make that dining room the stage on which your play will come to life. But don't feel you are limited to just the dining room; sometimes a bar area or lobby can become part of the setting.

First examine the room(s) and meet with the restaurant manager. Determine where and when you want the play's action to start. Will the play begin when the guests check in at the door or after they are seated? Will the action take place in the dining room only or will some of the play happen outside on a patio?

Also check on seating arrangements. Will some of your "characters" be dining with the audience? If so, additional chairs and meals will be needed for the actors that will be strategically placed throughout the room. For a more interactive environment, check out the distance between tables. Is it too crowded? Should tables be farther apart so the actors have more room to walk or run around them? (Remember that when people are seated, the chairs stick out even farther.) Do you want to create a theater-in-the-round by eliminating tables from the room's center? Where space is concerned, don't leave anything to chance.

Restaurant owners and managers are in the food business and don't always understand what is required for a smooth-running theatrical performance. You don't want to be moving tables and changing the actors' seating minutes before opening night.

Once you and the manager have agreed on the space requirements and number of tables, draw a sketch of the floor plan and indicate the areas where the play's action will take place. Give a copy of the sketch to the manager to guard against any surprises.

The Script

Many original scripts in this genre contain mainly character and action descriptions and serve primarily as an improvisational guide for the actor. Most of the speaking lines contained within it can be paraphrased by the actors as long as its meaning is understood by the audience.

However, you should mark any dialogue in the script that should be recited exactly as written. Reasons for this vary. There may be certain clues that need to be conveyed in a particular way to the audience in order for them to solve the mystery. Perhaps characters need specific language to explain who they are or how they feel about another character. (If you get your script from a royalty house, make sure you know what changes you can make without violating the terms of your agreement.)

The Actors

Performing in audience-participation theater tends to be an unsettling experience for even seasoned actors. Most of the comfort zones found in traditional stage plays are all but gone in the interactive setting. There is no protective fourth wall, no dimming of house lights, and often no cue lines. The actor is in direct contact with the audience members, sometimes drafting them to play parts in a scene.

During rehearsals, the director needs to foster an atmosphere of creativity and encouragement by helping the actors become more comfortable with the improvisational nature of the show and assisting them in discovering and playing their characters' objectives.

It all begins with the readthrough. Allow each actor to read his or her own character description so the other actors begin to identify who that actor will be portraying. Have the actors take turns reading the actions. Any dialogue, though, should be read by the actor who will be saying that particular line in performance.

Tell the actors not to "act" as they are reading and to simply listen to the play. After a short break, have them read through the script again. Distribute copies of the floor plan and a flowchart of the major actions in the play. This chart will assist the actors in becoming familiar with the order and progression of the play's action.

Use the next rehearsal to free the actors by doing some improvisational exercises. A good one is "group therapy," where all the actors, in character, sit in a circle and discuss their lives, relationships, problems, and motivations. Urge each actor to play the character's objective and encourage animated responses. Keep it free-flowing and alive.

During the remaining rehearsals, get the play on its feet and running. Block your actors so they are visible to most of the audience. Make sure the actors can be heard in all the room's nooks and crannies and that the play's pacing moves swiftly. At the last rehearsal, put the actors' improvisational skills to the test by bringing in some friends or family members to form an audience. Seat them in different locations in the room so the actors become accustomed to moving around to all corners of the space. Because of the improvisational nature of the play, no more than a half-dozen rehearsals are necessary. This will retain the spontaneity and energy of the performances.

When opening night rolls around, remind your actors to stay in character, be prepared for the unexpected, and have fun.

The Cutting Edge

The Pitfalls—and Secrets—of Editing a Script for Competition

43

W hen Shakespeare wrote of the "poor player that struts and frets his hour upon the stage," he was speaking of human mortality.

But that brief hour on stage is a fact of life at drama competitions, where entries must obey strict time constraints. Typical is a sixty-minute performance time, plus ten minutes to set up and another ten minutes to strike. Given these restrictions, one might assume that one-act plays would be the norm. Not so, as it turns out. Many plays seen in competition are edited versions of full-length scripts.

That's why we asked three well-known adjudicators— *Stage Directions* consultant Mortimer Clark, Brid McBride, and Annette Procunier—to talk about how best to edit a play for festival performance.

Interestingly enough, all three believe that if given the choice, it would be better to do a one-act play or one act of a longer play, rather than cut down a full-length script. (This may come as a surprise to those who think there is a competitive advantage to doing a well-known play edited for competition.) They have some wise counsel about finding quality plays of an appropriate length. However, recognizing that cutting will occur, they also explain how to do it with the least amount of damage to the original.

Cut to the Quick

The bottom line, the three judges say, is that if a playwright had intended on writing a sixty-minute script, he or she would have done so. A play is an organic whole—cut any part of it, and it's no longer that play. It's far better to pick a script that can be done within the competition's time frame.

"There are loads of good one-act plays," McBride says. "People really ought to be looking there first. Or do one act of a longer play."

Clark agrees. "I think the second act of *Absurd Person Singular* is the best 'one-act' play there is," Clark adds. "It doesn't really relate to Acts One and Three. It makes a great choice for competition. There are a number of other plays that have a strong act that can be performed alone."

Even if doing one act means just letting the play stop without a climax, Procunier says, "You'll be fine if you let the audience know what you're doing. What they want to see is how well you perform the material you've chosen."

McBride points out that the concept of cutting plays for competition is an American phenomenon. "In Europe, especially in Ireland where I work, you are required to do a one-act play. Nobody cuts a word. No playwright would allow it."

Clark and McBride say international festivals are an excellent place to find new short plays that have not been done to death in America. Another source is Actors Theatre of Louisville's annual Humana Festival, which features short plays from new and established playwrights.

Surviving the Cut

Realistically, however, the three judges realize editing a play for length is common in festival competition. So if you *must* cut, how can you do so with the least damage to the original?

"First," points out Procunier, "you need to ask whether the play *can* be cut, legally. Some playwrights forbid it; it's in the contract you sign. Be sure to clear all cuts with the publisher.

"Second, even if you have the legal right to cut, you have to ask whether it makes artistic sense to do so. Some plays are simply too long or too complex to shorten to an hour. They're so tightly organized, cutting robs them of their strength."

One common problem is a cutting that preserves the plot but not essentials, such as character development or theme.

"You have to be true to the playwright," says McBride. "And if you cut a long, poetic show—like *J.B.*, for example—it loses so much in the cutting, and I've seen it done with pages cut out of it. What's important about *J.B.*, isn't the story, but rather the way that MacLeish the poet transforms the biblical account of Job into modern terms, using verse. When you edit the verse, you strip away the logic that binds the play together."

Cutting Corners

"Have a clear understanding of why a line, scene, or character exists before cutting," director James A. Van Leishout writes. "Whether it's topicality, repetition, or stage conventions and logistics, your understanding of the function of a scene, line, or character can aid in cutting."

The best way to cut is to remove many small pieces rather than huge chunks of text, our three judges say.

"Read the script out loud and listen for the repetitious elements that can be cut out," McBride says, "as well as side comments, things that don't add anything to the play. Then go through it again and keep pruning out small pieces that aren't necessary. But make sure you maintain the continuity of the story."

This means the director needs to read the script many times, be very familiar with all of it, know what is essential to an understanding not only of the plot, but of the characters, and of course, the author's intent.

"Then you need to ask yourself, does this version make sense?" McBride says. "Will the audience understand it if they haven't seen the play before? Because your cutting must stand on its own."

Clark agrees. "Repetitious words are a good place to start, especially the use of names. Once a person is named, that is enough. And some playwrights are easier to cut than others. Shaw repeats a lot, so saying something once is usually enough. Wilde needs little trimming. Just make sure when you do cut speeches that you allow them to end naturally. Don't let them trail off, which is the sign of a bad edit."

Procunier's advice: "Keep the subtext, the sense *between* the lines, as it were. And watch for scenes and transitions that are essential for character development and sense."

Cutting Remarks

Removing repetitious or unnecessary words or phrases can shorten a play without hacking out huge chunks of exposition or character development, as in this example from Maxwell Anderson's *Elizabeth the Queen*:

> CECIL: You have a poor estimate of me, Master Bacon. If you go in to the queen and reveal to her that her letters to Essex have not reached him . . . as you mean to do . . . the queen will then send for me, and I will send for Lord Essex's last letter to you, containing a plan for the capture of the City of London. It will interest you to know that I have read that letter and you are learned enough in the law to realize in what light you will stand as a witness should the queen see it.
>
> BACON: I think it is true, though, that if I go down, I shall also drag a few with me, including those here present.
>
> CECIL: I am not so sure of that either. I am not unready for that contingency. But to be frank with you, it would be easier for both you and us if you were on our side.

Contrast that with:

> CECIL: You have a poor estimate of me. If you reveal that her letters to Essex have not reached him, the queen will send for me, and I will send for Lord Essex's last letter to you, containing a plan for the capture of the City of London. You are learned enough to realize in what light you will stand should the queen see it.
>
> BACON: If I go down, I shall also drag a few with me, including those present.
>
> CECIL: I am not unready for that contingency. To be frank with you, it would be easier for both you and us if you were on our side.

The Final Picture
How to Stage an Effective Curtain Call

44

*I*t's a pain to stage, and often is left until the last possible moment. But your production's curtain call is far too important to be treated as an afterthought. On the contrary, it deserves the same creative thought and planning as the play that precedes it. After all, it is the final stage picture the audience sees before it leaves the theater.

It also signals the end of this particular theatergoing experience, acting as an important transition between the world of the play and the real world to which the audience is returning.

And, of course, it gives the audience a chance to show its appreciation for the performance as a whole, and to individual performers in particular.

Understanding these three elements is essential to creating an effective curtain call. So are these four rules of thumb: keep it building to a climax, keep it moving, keep it interesting, then clear the stage. Here's how you can put these rules into action.

1. *Keep It Building.* Generally speaking, the script dictates the order in which the actors appear, from the least important characters to the most important. Often, you'll find that

during the course of rehearsal, the relative importance of characters to the production becomes clearer—a good reason for waiting to block bows until the last runthrough before technical rehearsals.

Begin by grouping together all those with no lines or without distinguishing characters—the chorus in a musical, for example, or the townspeople in *Cyrano de Bergerac.*

Next bring on the bit players—those with one or two lines— again as a group. Follow with the supporting players, in groups of two, three, or four related characters.

Finally, the lead players, giving each a solo bow, working toward the central character. If there are two central characters, as in *The Taming of the Shrew,* bring on the two actors together, then let each take a bow, first to the other, and then to the audience.

Finally, have the entire company take a bow, and close the curtain.

2. *Keep It Moving.* Overlap all stage movement. An individual or group walks quickly downstage to receive applause, and as soon as they are in position and begin bowing, the next group or individual should begin its way down, and so on with each successive bow. This may take some rehearsal, but the result is worth it. The energy on stage will be matched by that of the audience.

Movement is especially important in a musical, where bows normally have their own music. A good musical director will have additional music ready, but it's better if the cast keeps on track. Rehearse bows to the music, so the actors know their cue. That way, if someone slows down, the next person can pick up the pace, knowing where their bow should begin in the score.

3. *Keep It Interesting.* Creating an effective final picture means paying attention to how people are grouped on the stage. Build the stage picture throughout the call, adding groups and levels from backstage to front. If there are platforms or stairs, place actors on them after they finish their bow. This not only adds variety to the picture, but also lets the audience see everyone on stage.

You also can use groups to underscore the ensemble nature of a show. For a production of *Morning's at Seven,* a director blocked everyone to enter at the same time. Two family groups stood or sat on their respective back porch and steps; another pair sat on a stage-left stump; another stood stage right. No one was center stage. This kept the focus on the ensemble, and still allowed the audience to applaud.

However, if you're building to a final solo bow, such as in *Hello,*

Dolly! or *King Lear,* design the curtain call so the groupings gradually frame a downstage-center position, into which the lead actor walks. (Make sure the character merits this focus; otherwise, a sense of anticlimax will ruin the effect.)

The group bow at the end of the curtain call should be rehearsed so everyone bows as one. The simplest method is to trigger it by someone in the front row who is visible to everyone on stage. This person begins by first tilting his head back slightly, so when he bends forward, the rest of the cast is with him.

In a musical, the cast also should acknowledge the conductor, who then asks the orchestra to stand. The cast should join in the applause for the musicians. A final group bow should follow to reframe the stage picture.

4. *Get off the Stage.* Keep curtain calls as brief as possible. The audience wants to acknowledge the performers, but it doesn't want to make a night of it. Besides, clapping for more than a few minutes is tiring. Even if the audience stamps, applauds, and continues to yell "Bravo!," fade the lights, drop the curtain, bring up the houselights, and go home. You've earned the rest.

Curtainless Calls ■ Blocking most curtain calls is fairly straightforward. However, some situations present special challenges.

For example, if your play is presented without a curtain, creating a stage picture must be done in full view of the audience. Even if the cast returns in a blackout, they can be seen getting into position.

The curtain call for *Morning's at Seven,* described previously, was done without a curtain. When the lights came back up, the cast entered from the various houses or from off stage. In a production of *She Loves Me,* the director had the lovers walk off the stage, arm in arm, followed by a slow fade except for a single street lamp illuminating the exterior of the perfumery. As the lights came back up, the cast returned to the stage through the perfumery door to accept the applause.

For *Once Upon a Mattress*, a director kept Winifred asleep in bed, with the returning cast forming a picture around her. Prince Dauntless made one last futile attempt to awaken her. Illuminated by a follow spot, she attempted to sit up, then sank back in sleep, to much applause (and laughter).

In each case, the curtain call's blocking was suggested by the set itself, providing a satisfying conclusion to the performance. Look to your own set for similar ideas when staging a curtainless call.

True to Life ■ In general, actors should take the curtain call as themselves, not as their character. As a director has told us, "The play is over. The characters no longer exist."

This said, it must be acknowledged that some plays may call for a different approach. For a production of *The Crucible*, the director felt uncomfortable in bringing back John Proctor just after he had been executed. Instead, she posed the cast in related groups, then opened the curtain, with each group silhouetted in the harsh light of a separate spotlight. They remained motionless for the final picture, underscored by the sound of drums; then the lights faded and the curtain closed.

In a production of *Suddenly, Last Summer*, however, a similar approach backfired. The shortness of the single-act play and the enigmatic nature of the final line left most members of the audience puzzled. They didn't applaud because they didn't know the play was over until the houselights came up. There was no transition from the world of the play to the real world, cheating both audience and actors of needed closure. Bows would have helped.

Whatever your choice, make sure *all* players appear either as themselves or in character. In a production one of our editors saw recently, everyone took bows as themselves except for one actor. By staying in character, he seemed to be begging for attention. ("Hey, remember me? I'm the crusty old guy with the limp!")

Final Thoughts

1. *Keep the focus.* Audiences sometimes respond more to effort than artistry, and some players may receive a bigger hand than their work deserves. For example, a cute player can get a bigger hand than a more competent but restrained lead. And actresses who cry or die on stage often get more than their share of applause. Supporting players with flashy roles may get a bigger reaction than the leads. If you think this may be the case in your production, and you want to give everyone in the cast equal recognition, you can (a) present only a company bow; (b) block the cast into large groups of related characters and have each group take a bow together; or (c) put the audience favorite in a group of three featured players.

2. *Plan carefully*. Even spontaneous displays such as presenting flowers to the leading lady or calling the director on stage for a bow should be planned. In fact, prepare and rehearse *anything* that takes place within the existing curtain-call time.

3. *Stick to your guns.* Because of the obvious order of least-important characters to most important, not everyone will be happy with their lot. Don't change the curtain call to placate an actor, however. Explain the order of the bows, perhaps, but let it go at that. And don't change the curtain call once it's blocked and set. The cast doesn't need new blocking after opening night.

4. *Put some teeth into it.* For some reason, many actors don't smile during bows. Perhaps it's modesty. Perhaps it's fatigue. Whatever the reason, remind them to keep smiling. The audience wants to believe that all of those on stage have enjoyed themselves. Smiles encourage more applause too.

45 | Did You Know?

*E*ach issue of *Stage Directions* features tips on a wide range of subject matter. Here are some of those about directing that we've published since 1988.

By the Numbers

Along with your rehearsal schedule, include a wallet-sized piece of paper with important phone numbers that can be slipped into the cast member's wallet or purse. List a number where cast members can call to leave messages and the numbers of the director and stage manager, the theater (backstage), and the box office.

It's in the Book

Develop a delegation book. Whenever you delegate something to someone, mark it down in the book. This way you periodically can follow up on those things you've delegated and make sure all is going well.

Tape It

Instead of writing down your director's notes during a rehearsal, you can use a small, hand-held tape recorder. Reason: You can talk faster than you (or an assistant, if you have one) can write. Once the notes are recorded, you can transcribe them to be posted the next day, where the cast can see them before rehearsing again. If you prefer to give notes immediately after rehearsal, attach a headphone to the recorder and listen to the playback, using the pause button to advance to each taped note in sequence.

Electronic Accompaniment

With the price of a good piano equalling that of some cars, many groups that produce musicals are looking for alternatives. Taped music does not work well in most cases because it does not consider the fact that audience reaction or other causes may force the actor/singer to slow down or speed up. One answer to the dilemma might seem to be one of the new low-priced electronic keyboards, but these give the musician little flexibility. On the other hand, electronic pianos may prove to be a viable option. These respond to the force with which the player touches the keys (just like an acoustic piano) and offer a choice of several piano, harpsichord, and pipe-organ voices. They come with optional foot pedals, for sustained sections, and stands to raise them to playing level. They are portable, compact, easy to store, and do not slip out of tune with changes in the weather. The only major drawback is that the keyboard is shorter, usually with sixty-one keys rather than the eighty-eight of a conventional piano.

What's So Funny?

Sometimes seventeenth- and eighteenth-century comedies are directed as if they were pure old comedy farce. This shows a lack of common sense and a sloppy job of research. Moliere's plays, for example, are farcical, but they are also social satires. His characters may at times act ridiculous or approach slapstick, but they also should be believably multidimensional human beings.

Floored

When stage time is not available for rehearsals and scenes must be rehearsed in other spaces, preset stage diagrams drawn to scale allow you to lay out the exact dimensions of a scene using a measuring tape and masking tape. However, physical objects such as furniture are best used to indicate flats or walls. Actors tend to move closer to the taped lines or even step over them, and later feel cramped when they move onto the actual set. Care in setting up the makeshift rehearsal area helps avoid the frustration of reblocking on the actual stage set.

Write It Down

A rehearsal log is an excellent way to keep track of many things, including the answer to the question, "How did we ever get ourselves into this predicament, anyway?" In a looseleaf notebook—perhaps the one in which you keep the working script—dedicate a sheet of notepaper for each rehearsal. You might include such information as cast members who are late or absent, cast changes, scenes that were blocked or run and the number of times they were run, delays and causes, any failure to run a scheduled scene, and any out-of-the-ordinary event such as an accident, mechanical problem, or argument. You can use the log to keep track of miscellaneous items for follow-up, such as a needed prop or change in costume. A log also comes in handy when doing a post-mortem on the production; it's easy to forget all the bits and pieces that go into making a show.

Separate but Equal

Sometimes it's best to rehearse an actor separately when introducing complicated bits of business. Working out such details in public can cause feelings of inadequacy and undermine confidence. It also can hold up rehearsal.

Acting with Sole

To capture the appropriate walk and posture of the characters they are portraying, ask actors to wear character shoes in rehearsal and make use of all costume accessories. They are part of the action and help define their character.

Keep It Simple

In improvisations, the simplest subjects give the actor the most scope. The aim is to use imagination to investigate a particular subject. Avoid detailed or elaborate scenarios and let the actors bring any additional complexity to the subject they want.

Keep Your Eyes Open

Many actors unconsciously reveal their own attitudes to the characters. A director should watch for those who invite an audience to laugh at them in a comedy or who play for sympathy in a serious play. The solution is to clarify the action of the sequence with the actor. Look at the text with the actor and decide what the character *does*. Then decide *how* and the way in which the *how* can be expressed in action. If he or she plays it properly, there will be little time for anything else and the performance will be cleaner.

Tech Tip

When you encounter problems in technical rehearsals, give priority to those that affect performers—costume and scene changes and props. One simple reason is that lighting and scenery problems can be solved more easily when no one else is around. More importantly, however, actors need to gain confidence in their use of props and costumes and with how set changes will affect their entrances and exits. Once secure in this, an actor can concentrate on giving a good performance.

Sound Advice

If you are going to use a number of prerecorded sound effects in a play, it's a good idea to have a rough tape to be used in rehearsals so you as well as the actors and stage manager all get used to working with the sound cues. The rehearsal tape can be done quite simply, without the fine-tuning that will be needed for performance. The rehearsal tape also will help ensure that cues are appropriate.

"Line!"

Prompters at rehearsals should try to look at the actors as often as possible while following the text with the fingers. If the prompters read along without glancing up, their tendency will be to prompt every time there is a pause. Some actors may ask for a prompt. Others will not want to break out of character and may just look up in your direction. Every time there is a silence, look up at the actors to see whether they are acting or have really dried up. Mark all acting pauses in the script to remind yourself not to prompt at these moments.

High School Tip

The director of high school theater should keep coaches and activity advisors informed of those students cast in a production or working backstage, along with a rehearsal and performance schedule. You'll find that this kind of thoughtfulness is appreciated and allows others to plan around your rehearsals.

What's in a Word?

About two-thirds of the way through rehearsal, a director may want to call a "word rehearsal." The cast sits comfortably and speaks the dialogue quietly. There should be no attempt to project. The object is to think about the play as a whole and to think about it in detail. Not having to project or move around, the actors listen more carefully to the play and to each other. Some actors close their eyes to concentrate even more on the language. Often, directors find this type of rehearsal brings new insights and subtleties to a performance.

Hands Off

When an actor gestures too much, try this. Tell the actor to put his hands in his pockets and stand with a book on his head. You'll find that all the energy that was going into movement now goes into line delivery. Now have him repeat the exercise, allowing just three gestures. Many actors will immediately feel the benefit of this exercise. However, they will soon revert to old habits if you don't watch them. Technique isn't acquired easily.

Roundabout

In blocking a play on a proscenium-arch stage, it may help to block as though the production were staged in the round. This will add a three-dimensional depth to the grouping. At a later stage, you can clean up the grouping so there is no masking.

What Is Style?

John Gielgud once defined *style* in acting as "knowing what kind of play you're in." Different playwrights demand different styles from the actor. This is partly because the content of their plays differs widely, partly because each is writing in a different context—time, place, social situation—and partly because each playwright has a different idea of the manner in which he or she expects the actors to relate to the audience. The result, director Tyrone Guthrie once pointed out, is that an actor cannot successfully impersonate his or her character without quite drastic variations in both the imaginative and technical approaches.

Get Some Shut-Eye

Directors may want to listen to at least one rehearsal with eyes closed or back turned to the actors to judge how well the actors' voices command attention and interest.

Memory Aid

Before quitting for the day when working on a project, such as blocking a scene or preparing a report, write yourself a few notes on where you go next with the undertaking. That will make it much easier when you pick up the effort again.

Avoiding One-Upmanship

When dealing with a know-it-all, don't attempt to be a know-it-all in return. When you disagree with know-it-alls, they will immediately freeze their ideas and won't budge; then you've created a standoff. It's better to ask questions about the idea, since know-it-alls love to answer questions. As they look for answers, they might just discover that some ideas you present could be useful. In fact, they'll probably blend some of your ideas with theirs and think that they came up with all of them.

A Tight by Any Other Name . . .

Male performers balk at wearing tights? One high school instructor tells her male actors tights are just cycling shorts with feet, or the same garment football players wear under their uniform to keep warm.

Stay out of It

The Peoria Players Theatre recently invoked a new rule: Directors and choreographers cannot appear in their own shows. "As more new directors and choreographers start working with us," says President Gail Anderson, "we want to prevent the problems that are an almost inevitable result of trying to direct yourself. Having done it myself, I know that one finds oneself relying on other ears to evaluate the vocal balance. You can't give the other performers all your attention because you also have to hone your own performance. Other eyes have to watch the stage picture, or you have to step out of the stage picture and try to guess what the whole looks like when you're in it. And there's no one who can tell you if what you're doing as a performer is working or not." Exceptions can be made, but the director will have to petition the board, Anderson says.

Keep Them in the Dark

About a week before opening, "when tech rehearsals really start to get to you," Canadian director Ron Cameron puts his actors in a totally darkened room and runs lines. The result, he says, is that "they hear a play they really haven't heard in weeks." The exercise returns focus to the lines themselves, and the result, he believes, is a sharper performance.

What's That You Say?

Think twice about putting your director's notes in a printed program, advises theater professor and play adjudicator Mort Clark. "Notes about the origin of the play, the playwright, or the historical or social milieu can be helpful," he says, "but when a director feels he must explain his concept or what he thinks the play is about, it means he doesn't trust the audience—which is insulting—or he doesn't trust his directing ability—which is unsettling. The work should stand on its own."

A Potpourri

Thoughts on directing from theater professor and director Kent Brown.

- "If an actor is having problems with a scene, give him a prop or have him suggest a prop and have him use these during rehearsal. This will divert him from self-consciousness and help him focus."

■ "A line-perfect actor may not be a good actor. He may be reliable, but he also may be hiding behind the shield of the text."

■ "Take a look at where your characters are off-balance. Audiences don't pay money to watch balance and harmony in any play. They don't pay money to watch people do things easily."

■ "Look at the entrances and exits in your play. Plays are about leaving. Plays are about coming and arriving, about reconvening the human community."

Trippingly on the Tongue

Royal Shakespeare Company director Adrian Noble has devoted much attention to teaching his actors the special talent of speaking Shakespeare's verse properly. It's an art, he agrees, that some people believe impossible for an American actor to muster.

"It shouldn't be," he told Blake Green of the *San Francisco Chronicle*. "The kind of whole, wonderful energies inside the American accent and dialects should be good for Shakespeare. But you need to harness the rhythmical energy of Shakespeare to that accent, and for some reason that's difficult—maybe because American actors try to play naturalistic, the whole modern Stanislavsky tradition, and Shakespeare was writing for a very different kind of actor. He wouldn't have understood 'characterization,' having provided the information and the psychology of the character within the dialogue."

A Different Slant

Director Dianna Shuster, of San Jose's American Musical Theatre, believes that Sondheim wrote *A Little Night Music* in three-quarter time "not to prove he could do it—the conventional wisdom," but "because the show is basically about a ménage à trois." She used that idea in the staged overture, with groups of three actors waltzing together.

No Male Magnolias

It's often illegal to change the gender of characters in plays protected by copyright. A recent example was a production of *Steel Magnolias* in Memphis, in which the role of beauty-shop owner Truvy was to be played by a male—who just happened to be a professional hairdresser. Three weeks before opening night, Dramatists Play Service ordered the show's producer to recast the role with a woman or lose the rights to stage the play. Like many other playwrights (including Edward Albee and Tennessee Williams), Robert Harling would not permit the substitution on the grounds that it violated the artistic integrity of his play. "I have never checked with a publishing house on who I cast before," producer Jackie Nichols told the *New York Times.* "We do a lot of nontraditional casting here and we don't ask, for instance, if we can cast a black actor in a role traditionally played by a white person. So what is the difference here? Is one type of discrimination OK and another not?" Dramatists Play Service, like any royalty house, was simply carrying out the wishes of the author, as it is required to do. It's a good idea, therefore, to read the specifics of any royalty contract, many of which have specific bans on gender changes.